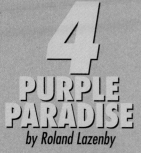

The **Gold Collectors** SERIES ™

Gold Collectors Series Sports Magazine

Michael M. Meyers	Publisher
Mike Morris	Managing Editor
Elliott From	Managing Art Director

Contributors

Roland Lazenby	Feature Writer
Allsport	Photos
AP/Wide World	Photos
Quad Graphics	Printing

Publishers of Quality Magazines
H&S MEDIA ™
INCORPORATED

2121 Waukegan Road, Bannockburn, IL 60015
Phone: (847) 444-4880 • Fax: (847) 444-1153

Distributed by Warner Publisher Services and
ADS Publisher Services, Inc.

H&S Media, Inc.

Harvey Wasserman	CEO
Steve Keen	President
Michael M. Meyers	Executive Vice President
Richard Pinder	Controller
Kathy Arthur	Purchasing Coordinator
Kimberly Blair	Production Coordinator
Jill Djuric	Corporate Imaging Manager
Rick Kieras	Scanner Operator
Patrick Julian	National Advertising Director

© 1998 Contents H&S Media, Inc., All Rights Reserved. Reproduction in whole or part by any means, including electronic, without the written permission of the publisher is strictly prohibited. "Gold Collectors Series" is a trademark of H&S Media, Inc.

Check out The Gold Collectors Series on the Internet!

http://www.gcsmag.com

Back orders of this magazine can be obtained by contacting:
Vikings: Road to the Super Bowl
ISI
30 Montgomery Street
Jersey City, NJ 07302
Phone: (800) 544-6748 Fax: (201) 451-5745
e-mail: isi@wwmag.com
The cost for a back ordered issue is the cover price of the issue + $2.50 postage and handling.

This publication is not sponsored or endorsed by the Minnesota Vikings or the National Football League. This is not an official publication.

PURPLE PARADISE

Revamped Vikings running roughshod over helpless foes

by Roland Lazenby

After staggering through a whirlwind of controversy, Dennis Green and his Minnesota Vikings are riding tall these days. Frankly, some folks don't seem to know what to make of the reversal of fortunes. Is this really an NFL franchise or just an HBO miniseries posing as one?

If you have trouble answering that one, you've obviously been reading only the headlines lately. If you bothered to dig into the fine print, you'd know that Green and his Vikings are most definitely for real. They've spent the 1998 regular season kicking serious booty in the NFC Central, and just about anywhere else the schedule has taken them.

With playoff dates approaching, Green and his Vikings were steamrolling their way to home-dome advantage in the NFC and unabashedly setting their sights on a Super Bowl ring. That, it seems, is the reward for renovating the defense and reinvigorating an old quarterback and stealing the game's offensive star of the future with the 21st pick of the draft.

Like that, Randy to Randy, Cunningham to Moss, has become the NFL's prime-time connection. Which means the Vikings have finally realized their identity as the league's most feared invaders; they're visiting visions of humiliation and embarrassment upon the heads of opponents Sunday after Sunday.

The numbers?

The Vikes raced to a 7-0 start and won 11 of their first dozen games, good enough to produce a virtual stranglehold on the NFC lead and their first Central Division title since 1994. The first prize of the season was their sixth playoff berth in seven seasons under Green, but this team clearly has more on its mind. And it seems to have the offense to get it. The Vikings' attack produced an NFC-high 394 points over the first dozen games, a hefty 32.8 points per game. Cunningham filled in for injured starter Brad Johnson by leading the league in passer rating, completing 61 percent of his passes for 2,565 yards and 23 touchdowns with just 7 interceptions through the first 12 contests.

This, of course, is the same Randall Cunningham who starred for years in Philadelphia as a big arm (with ego to match) yet was plainly skittish to bolt the pocket too early and too often. Despite a run of gutty performances and solid numbers over the years, his ultimate lack of success as an Eagle was emphasized by his forced retirement after the 1995 season. Quite

Roland Lazenby is the author of numerous sports books, including "Blood On The Horns; The Long Strange Ride of Michael Jordan's Chicago Bulls." His most recent title on the NFL is "Smashmouth."

simply, no other team wanted him.

Cunningham even managed to play in an old-timer's game before being called back to the league in 1997 by Green. Operating from the role of a graybeard backup, he has vaulted into MVP contention, mainly by dropping the ego and holding fast to the team concept. Mention his performance to Vikings wideout Cris Carter, who also played with Cunningham in Philadelphia, and you'll get whole paragraphs on the QB's newfound virtues.

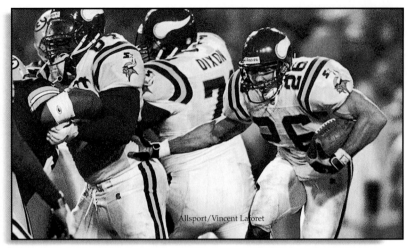
Allsport/Vincent Laforet

"Randall is far more mature then he was (in Philly)," Carter says. "I think he is at peace with himself and I think he really works on trying to be a good player and not necessarily just doing what people want him to do. He really sits back and looks at the weaknesses in his game and really tries to work on them and has really tried to work in our system to figure out where everyone is going to be at in certain situations and he is not as risky, as daring, pays a lot of attention to turnovers and taking care of the ball; has great presence in the pocket when people are around him. He is covering the ball up instead of trying to make one guy miss and trying to carry the team on his shoulders."

"It really helps when you have God in your heart and you focus on reading the Bible and studying what it says," explained Cunningham, who played the first 11 years of his career with the Eagles, "because it really has the answers to all the questions I've had in life."

"He has a great understanding of team concept that coach Dennis Green has implemented here with the Vikings and has really embraced the backup role for the Vikings which he would have never done in Philadelphia," Carter added. "He is great in the locker room as far as leadership with the younger players. Even when he is not playing, he is very consistent, as far as his personality on a day in, day out basis."

Yet it's hard to find a day when he's not playing. In November, he shook off the after effects of bone chip removal surgery and found a way to lead his team to victory over Cincinnati.

Of course it helps that for much of the season he's had the delight of targeting perhaps the finest three-man receiver corps in the history of games that involve playing catch. The addition of fab rookie Randy Moss to a crew that already included big producers Carter and Jake Reed forced Green to happily go with a three-receiver alignment. The result was a stretched playing field for opponents and a highway to high hopes for Deep Purple fans.

Just months ago, such a turn of events seemed impossible with the Vikings tripping through one unsavory circumstance after another. Heck, the main issue facing Green was how to hang onto his job for the last season of a five-year contract. The Vikings franchise was a virtual soap opera with more twists and fantastic turns than, say, a Tom Clancy novel.

Oops.

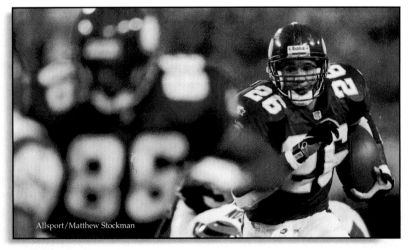
Allsport/Matthew Stockman

Therein, of course, lies much of the explanation to this mystery. The Vikings were a team without a majority owner, ruled instead by a 10-owner committee, a set of circumstances that has never, ever worked in professional sports (if you question that, just ask the Chicago Bulls about the misery of committee rule in their early days). In Minnesota, the situation grew so dire that Green penned an autobiography in 1997 that spelled out a proposal for him to purchase control of the team.

Allsport/Scott Halleran

Seething with chutzpah, the coach even threatened legal action against a couple of the team's owners. Not exactly what you'd call a formula for job security. Unless, of course, you happen to win. And somehow that's exactly what Green has managed to do, to the delight of his players and legions of Vikings fans.

VIKINGS HEADED BY A MAN NAMED RED – A NATURAL COMBINATION

At first, it seemed that Clancy, the author of a run of high-dollar military techno-thrillers, was poised to take over during the offseason, but suddenly Clancy's offer

to purchase the team for $200 million fell through when it became clear he didn't have the cash. In stepped that affable Texan, Red McCombs, former owner of the San Antonio Spurs and Denver Nuggets, who produced a $250 million offer that was hungrily slurped up by the Vikings' committee of owners, especially after McCombs assured Minnesota fans that he had no plans to move the Vikes to Texas.

Wasting little time after the NFL approved the sale in late August, McCombs secured the resignation of team president Roger Headrick, who had also sought to purchase the club. Headrick's last acts as prez, how-

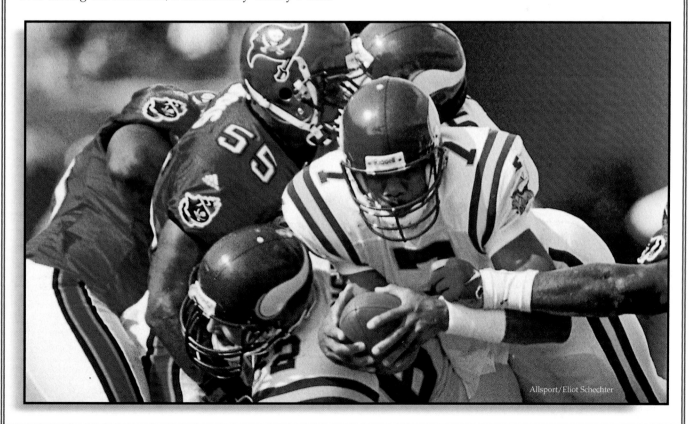

Allsport/Eliot Schechter

Allsport/Elsa Hasch

ever, proved to be a major assist. He spent big bucks on the future by paying to retain free agents Robert Smith, John Randle, Todd Steussie and Jake Reed.

With Headrick's departure, McCombs whipped out a three-year contract extension for Green just as the regular season was about to start. In retrospect, it made perfect sense, but at the time there were a host of critics pointing to the messy allegations strewn in Green's recent past, including a claim of sexual harassment. For others, the real issue was his track record of just one playoff win in six years.

For McCombs, though, the 49-year-old Green was clearly a winner (with a 56-40 record) and clearly in touch with the team, which finished 9-7 in 1997 and entered the playoffs as a wild-card team that upset the New York Giants in the first round with a dramatic rally over the final two minutes.

"I'm extremely excited and proud to continue in my capacity as the head coach of the Minnesota Vikings," Green said in response to the move. "Our coaching staff and players feel strong that this makes a great statement on Red McCombs' commitment for success now and in the future."

Certainly, it only seems fitting that a man named

Red should rule the Vikings. Better yet, his downhome style seems perfect for helping to heal the wounds that have staggered this franchise. One Minneapolis columnist even referred to McCombs as a "chicken-fried Moses," a comment that reportedly offended Green. Local reporters, however, point out that umbrage is one of the coach's trademark approaches in creating an "Us vs. Them" mentality to motivate his team. There is little question that Green and the Minnesota media have engaged in a running battle in recent seasons. Helping to ease those community tensions would prove to be one of McCombs' big chores. It helps that he's clearly promotions minded.

"He believes that the athletes on the Vikings should play a tremendous role in the community and he wants us to be a part of the community," Carter said of the new owner. "He wants us to get out and show people, not only are we good athletes, but we are also good citizens in that community."

Winning, of course, has always been the best community relations tool, and McCombs' swift move to extend Green's contract set the mood for that. "Success," as Green predicted, quickly became the operative word. The Vikings were brimming with talent and evidenced that by blistering through the pre-season with a 4-0 record.

"We feel like this is going to be our year," Green proclaimed as the regular season opened. "We've got a clear-cut goal for ourselves and that's to become the Super Bowl champions. We feel it's realistic. We feel it's attainable."

AN UPGRADED DEFENSE

To make serious talk of a Super Bowl run, Green knew that his 1998 club would have to be better than at the end of the 1997 season, when defensive coordinator Foge Fazio found himself starting four rookies: end Stalin Colinet, tackle Tony Williams, linebacker Dwayne Rudd, and free safety Torrian Gray. As a unit, the group had finished the season ranked 29th in the league.

Big, bad John Randle had been brought back to anchor the defensive line, but the development of the linebacker corp kept the coaches worried. Ed McDaniel moved inside to replace Jeff Brady and was joined by Rudd and Dixon Edwards. To add depth, the Vikings had drafted Kailee Wong, Kivuusama Mays, and Chester Burnett.

To bolster the secondary, they brought in former Patriot cornerback Jimmy Hitchcock to team with Corey Fuller. With safety Orlando Thomas slowly recovering from knee surgery, Gray was slated for playing time alongside strong safety Robert Griffith.

"We think we're going to have an improved pass rush," Green said when asked about his defense. "Duane Clemons is improved. John Randle is one of the top rushers in the league. We have Kailee Wong, a pick out of Stanford who can rush the passer. He'll play defensive line as well as at blitzing linebacker. We think those ingredients will help us become a better pass-

rush football team.

"And we think the secondary is better," the coach added. "We traded for Jimmy Hitchcock from the Patriots. He's a very confident player. Then we drafted Ramos McDonald, who's a good solid player. Then we have Orlando Thomas back healthy. He led the league in interceptions three years ago as a rookie. We feel he'll make a big difference."

On special teams the news was the dubious signing of 39-year-old place-kicker Gary Anderson from San Francisco to replace the oldest player in the NFL, 41-year-old Eddie Murray. Who could have figured that Anderson would turn in a career year and even make a push for a perfect season? It was just that kind

Allsport/Tom Pidgeon

of year in the Hubert H. Humphrey Metrodome. Joining Anderson were at least a dozen or more Vikings pushing for Pro Bowl honors.

The only thing threatening Minnesota's big ride was a run of injuries, but they served to emphasize this team's depth at virtually every position. Jake Reed, for example, fell victim to back surgery in November, but that didn't stop the Vikes from shoving one big play after another at the Dallas Cowboys over Thanksgiving, in Dallas no less. Carter had 7 catches for 135 yards, including a 54-yard score, and Moss caught 3 passes – all touchdowns – for 163 yards.

When the running game was hit by a November knee sprain for newly signed $25 million back Robert Smith, Green simply turned to tough old backup Leroy Hoard.

The offense kept chugging, mainly because of the addition of the incredible Moss. Green had taken a look at him at training camp and told reporters the offense has the chance to be "explosive" with the addition of the rookie.

Moss began proving him correct from the very first exhibition game, a win over New England that saw the 6-foot-4, 205-pounder pull in two catches for 54 yards and one touchdown.

The early scouting report from Patriots cornerback Ty Law? "The type of speed he has. I mean, he's a threat everytime he's on the field," he said of Moss.

A "threat" was all the Minnesota offense needed to gain lethal status. The Vikings zapped Tampa Bay, St. Louis, Detroit and Chicago to set up a Monday night showdown with the Packers in Green Bay in early October. Moss used the game as his coming out party with 190 yards of receiving yards and two touchdowns (Cunningham himself threw for 442 yards and 4 touchdowns, good enough for player of the week honors).

Much of Moss' production was generated by the rookie's 6-foot-4 height and indefensible combination of hops and speed.

"He's a big guy and has great leaping ability," Packers safety Darren Sharper said of Moss. "He doesn't play like a rookie, I'll tell you that."

That point was emphasized to the league as the

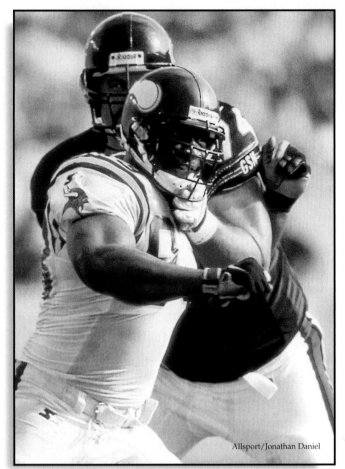

Allsport/Jonathan Daniel

Packers went down in flames and the Vikes took control of the division at 5-0. For what seemed like forever Minnesota had been bullied by Green Bay in Central races. But the 1998 regular season brought that to an end.

From there, they torched the Redskins 41-7 to go 6-0, their best start since 1975. Anderson extended his run of consecutive field goals to 18 straight with the outcome. The Purple defense sent its own message by sacking hapless Washington quarterbacks five times. "I think it says we're humble, we're hungry and we're not looking past anybody," said defensive end Duane Clemons, who had 1.5 sacks.

The next victim was Detroit on the road, finished off 34-13 with a third quarter run of 17 consecutive points. This time the ground game took the spotlight with Smith dashing to 134 yards on 19 carries, including a 57-yard touchdown run.

The joy ride hit a bump the next week in Tampa Bay when the Bucs were able to establish a ground game. Cunningham hit 21 of 25 passes for 291 yards and two TDs, but the Tampa Bay running game just kept churning. "It was one of those games where you have a shootout and whoever has the ball at the end of the game wins," Cunningham told reporters afterward. "They got the best of us today, but we humbly accept this loss and we'll just keep on going. It's not going to knock us down. It's not going to knock us out."

Far from it, the Vikings gutted out a 31-24 win against New Orleans back in Minnesota the next week, but it was costly. Cunningham injured his right knee and ankle early in the game, forcing Brad Johnson back into duty. He, too, was injured, sustaining a broken thumb.

By all rights Cunningham should have sat out the contest with Cincinnati the next week. But doctors removed the bone chips from his right knee six days before the game, and Cunningham removed the doubt, making just enough of an appearance to push the Vikes to a 9-1 record and a 24-3 win, highlighted by Dwayne Rudd's 63-yard fumble return.

The grit helped earn Cunningham the NFC Player of the Month honors for October. But observers were also beginning to credit a Vikings defense that had shut down reigning MVP Brett Favre and just about every other QB they'd faced. Through 10 games, Minnesota had allowed the second fewest points in the NFC (170) and was tied for second in the NFC with 14 interceptions. In their five home wins, the defense had given up just 47 points.

"We just keep growing as a defense,'" said Corey Fuller. "We keep believing. It's all believing to me."

That believability factor soared the next week when they plugged Green Bay again, the first time in five years that Minnesota had swept the regular season series from the Packers. The 28-14 win didn't mean that Packers coach Mike Holmgren was willing to concede Minnesota was the better team. "It doesn't matter.

It's irrelevant," Green said. "The bottom line is that playing Green Bay is just one step in the direction we want to go this year. We've played them twice, we've beat them twice. We'll probably play them again ... The only thing that really counts is who's going to be champions."

"I think we're just a really determined football team," Defensive end Derrick Alexander told reporters. "We had to go through those years of adjusting and getting guys where they needed to be and getting everybody here. Everybody's just starting to be comfortable around each other. That's something you have to do to be a championship team, and I think this year we're starting to blend a little bit."

That attitude further evidenced itself in the Thanksgiving win over the Cowboys just days after the Packer defeat. Once again, Moss stepped into the limelight. He caught just three passes against the Cowboys, but those three catches totaled 163 yards and all three went for touchdowns. "He might just be the best receiver in the game. He's the real deal," said former Cowboys wide receiver Drew Pearson.

If so, the same could be said of the Minnesota offense, as in REAL quick. Thirty-two of the Vikings' 44 touchdown drives over the season had taken less than three minutes, with 23 of those under two minutes and 12 under a minute.

"I've never been around this much firepower," said tight end Andrew Glover, "with a team that had the ability to strike at any time, from any place on the field."

That, of course, is just the way Dennis Green said it would be. Thank goodness Red was willing to listen. ∎

Allsport/Jonathan Daniel

WALK

Allsport/Jonathan Daniel

December 6, 1998 at Minneapolis
Vikings 48, Bears 22

Randy Moss set a single-season rookie record for touchdown receptions as the Minnesota Vikings continued to roll, jumping out to a 27-point half-time lead and clinching the NFC Central title with a 48-22 rout of the Chicago Bears on Sunday night.

Moss caught three more touchdown passes from Randall Cunningham, finishing with eight receptions for 106 yards. The star wideout set a new NFL record for first-year players with 14 TD catches, one better than John Jefferson of the 1979 San Diego Chargers and Billy Howton of the 1952 Green Bay Packers. It was the second straight week that Moss, a lock to win Rookie of the Year, pulled in three TDs. On Thanksgiving, he had three touchdowns – all for more than 50 yards – in a 46-36 win over Dallas. He is the first rookie since 1960 to go over 100 yards receiving in three straight games.

Cunningham was 21-of-31 for 349 yards as the Vikings clinched their first division title since 1994. They ended the three-year NFC Central reign of the Packers and remained one game in front of Atlanta for home-field advantage throughout the postseason. The Vikings tied a franchise record with their 12th win of the season, a mark previously reached four times under former coach Bud Grant.

Leroy Hoard started in place of injured halfback Robert Smith and had one touchdown rushing and another receiving.

The bad news for the Vikings was the loss of superstar wide receiver Cris Carter, who suffered a strained right calf in the opening minutes and saw his streak of consecutive games with a reception end at 111, a run which began November 3, 1991.

Gary Anderson kicked field goals of 30 and 20 yards to build a 20-0 Vikings lead. Anderson has hit all 23 of his attempts this season and 28 in a row overall, three shy of the all-time record set by former Viking Fuad Reveiz from 1994-95.

AP/Jim Mone

	1	2	3	4	F
Chicago Bears	0	0	14	8	22
Minnesota Vikings	14	13	7	14	48

First Quarter
Minnesota–Randy Moss 6-yard TD pass from Randall Cunningham (Gary Anderson kick)
Minnesota– LeRoy Hoard 24-yard TD pass from Randall Cunningham (Gary Anderson kick)

Second Quarter
Minnesota–Gary Anderson 30-yard FG
Minnesota–Gary Anderson 20-yard FG
Minnesota–Randy Moss 3-yard TD pass from Randall Cunningham (Gary Anderson kick)

Third Quarter
Chicago–Bobby Engram 47-yard TD pass from Steve Stenstrom (Jeff Jaeger kick)
Minnesota–Randy Moss 34-yard TD pass from Randall Cunningham (Gary Anderson kick)
Chicago–Edgar Bennett 5-yard TD run (Jeff Jaeger kick)

Fourth Quarter
Minnesota–LeRoy Hoard 8-yard TD run (Gary Anderson kick)
Minnesota–Dwayne Rudd 94-yard fumble return for TD (Gary Anderson kick)
Chicago–Steve Stenstrom 4-yard TD run (Steve Stenstrom pass to Chris Penn for 2-point conversion)

	Bears	Vikings
First Downs	19	23
Rushing	4	7
Passing	13	14
Penalty	2	2
Rushes-Yards	24-67	27-109
Average Per Rush	2.8	4.0
Comp-Att-Int	25-42-1	21-31-1
Net Passing Yards	272	349
Sacks-Yards Lost	3-31	0-0
Average Per Pass Play	6.0	11.3
Return Yards	119	92
Int Ret-Yds	1-2	1-0
Punt Ret-Yds	1-8	5-41
Kick Return Yards	4-109	3-51
Punts-Average	6-46.5	2-44.0
Fumbles Lost	1-1	0-0
Penalties-Yards	5-65	10-123
Time of Possession	31:17	28:43

RUSHING
CHICAGO: Bennett 12-21, Hallock 3-17, Stenstrom 4-15, Allen 4-11, Engram 1-3.
MINNESOTA: Hoard 19-69, Cunningham 1-19, Palmer 2-13, Evans 3-10, Fiedler 2(-2).
PASSING
CHICAGO: Stenstrom 25-42-1-303 yards.
MINNESOTA: Cunningham 21-31-1-349.
RECEIVING
CHICAGO: Engram 9-140, Conway 4-44, Bennett 3-34, Penn 3-32, Hallock 3-6, Allen 2-36, Mayes 1-11.
MINNESOTA: Moss 8-106, Hoard 4-63, Hatchette 3-26, Glover 2-55, Williams 1-64, Walsh 1-25, Delong 1-6, Palmer 1-4.
FUMBLES/LOST
CHICAGO: Stenstrom.
INTERCEPTIONS
CHICAGO: Harris 1-2.
MINNESOTA: Hitchcock 1-0

Attendance: 64,247

AP/Tom Olmscheid

AP/Tom Olmscheid

November 26, 1998 at Dallas
Vikings 46, Cowboys 36

Randall Cunningham threw four touchdown passes against a Dallas secondary without injured Deion Sanders, including three to rookie phenom Randy Moss, as the Vikings practically clinched first place in the NFC Central with a 46-36 Thanksgiving Day victory over the Cowboys.

One more Vikings victory or Green Bay loss will wrap up the division title for Minnesota, which has an NFC-best record of 11-1.

Cunningham completed 17-of-35 for 359 yards; Carter caught seven passes for 135 yards. Moss caught just three passes, but all three went for touchdowns, two 56-yarders and another for 51. He also drew a 50-yard interference penalty that set up another score. Cunningham also had a 54-yard TD pass to Cris Carter.

LeRoy Hoard filled in for the injured Robert Smith and had 12- and 50-yard touchdowns as Dallas allowed the fourth-most points in franchise history and the most since Minnesota scored 54 in 1970. Moss outran double-coverage for his 51-yard touchdown on a flea-flicker. Smith took the handoff and pitched back to Cunningham, who found Moss for the score. Minnesota got a 45-yard field goal from Gary Anderson just before the half ended for a 24-12 lead. Robert Smith sprained his knee in the first half and missed the rest of the game.

Emmitt Smith's third touchdown of the game, a 4-yarder, came with 1:06 left and tied him with Marcus Allen for first on the career rushing touchdown list with 123. Dallas also got a career-high 455 yards from Troy Aikman.

AP/Tim Sharp

	1	2	3	4	F
Minnesota Vikings	21	3	15	7	46
Dallas Cowboys	6	6	10	14	36

First Quarter
Minnesota—(1:57) Randy Moss 51-yard TD pass from Randall Cunningham (Gary Anderson kick)
Dallas—(5:25) Richie Cunningham 30-yard FG
Minnesota—(7:43) Cris Carter 54-yard TD pass from Randall Cunningham (Gary Anderson kick)
Dallas—(11:56) Richie Cunningham 46-yard FG
Minnesota—(12:19) Randy Moss 56-yard TD pass from Randall Cunningham (Gary Anderson kick)

Second Quarter
Dallas—(12:28) Patrick Jeffers 67-yard TD pass from Troy Aikman (Pass Failed)
Minnesota—(14:44) Gary Anderson 45-yard FG

Third Quarter
Dallas—(6:05) Emmitt Smith 2-yard TD run (Richie Cunningham kick)
Minnesota—(8:33) Leroy Hoard 12-yard TD run (Randy Moss 2-point conversion pass from Randall Cunningham)
Dallas—(13:40) Richie Cunningham 47-yard FG
Minnesota—(14:54) Randy Moss 56-yard TD pass from Randall Cunningham (Gary Anderson kick)

Fourth Quarter
Dallas—(6:12) Emmitt Smith 1-yard TD run (Richie Cunningham kick)
Minnesota—(7:27) Leroy Hoard 50-yard TD run (Gary Anderson kick)
Dallas—(13:54) Emmitt Smith 4-yard TD run (Richie Cunningham kick)

	Vikings	Cowboys
First Downs	21	31
Rushing	7	9
Passing	11	18
Penalty	3	4
Rushes-Yards	19-118	24- 58
Average Per Rush	6.2	2.4
Comp-Att-Int	17-35-1	34-57-0
Net Passing Yards	353	455
Sacks-Yards Lost	1-6	0-0
Average Per Pass Play	9.8	8.0
Return Yards	0	17
Int Ret-Yds	0-0	1-6
Punt Ret-Yds	1-0	1-11
Kick Return Yards	7-149	6-140
Punts-Average	4-38.3	4-44.0
Fumbles-Lost	2-0	2-0
Penalties-Yards	11-78	13-152
Time of Possession	21:57	38:03

RUSHING
MINNESOTA: Hoard 5-58, Smith 8-46, Cunningham 3-8, Evans 3-6.
DALLAS: Smith 18-44, Williams 4-8, Aikman 2-6.
PASSING
MINNESOTA: Cunningham 17-35-1-359.
DALLAS: Aikman 34-57-0-455.
RECEIVING
MINNESOTA: Carter 7-135, Moss 3-163, Evans 2-17, Hoard 2-11, DeLong 2-9, Glover 1-24.
DALLAS: Irvin 10-137, Johnston 5-21, Davis 4-70, Smith 4-30, Jeffers 3-92, LaFleur 3-30, Williams 2-43, Bjornson 2-25, Ogden 1-7.
FUMBLES/LOST
MINNESOTA: Williams 1-0, Palmer 1-0.
DALLAS: Smith 1-0, Ogden 1-0.
INTERCEPTIONS
MINNESOTA: None.
DALLAS: Reese 1-6.

Attendance: 64,366

AP/LM Otero

AP/Tim Sharp

November 22, 1998 at Minneapolis
Vikings 28, Packers 14

Randall Cunningham and Randy Moss teamed up again Sunday to lead Minnesota over the Green Bay Packers 28-14 to all but clinch the NFC Central.

The Vikings' defense did a number as well, putting Minnesota up 10-0 before the offense even had a first down. The victory put the Vikings (10-1) three games ahead of Green Bay (7-4) in the NFC Central with just five games remaining, as the Vikings also clinched at least a wild-card berth. Minnesota also won the tiebreaker over the Packers because it won the first meeting, 37-24 at Green Bay.

The Vikings were propelled by the defense in this game: Jimmy Hitchcock's 58-yard interception return and Gary Anderson's field goal following Tony Williams' fumble recovery gave Minnesota a quick 10-0 lead.

The win was highlighted by Moss' performance. Might might very well have solidified his hold on offensive rookie of the year honors with eight catches for 153 yards, plus a 61-yard reception negated by a penalty. Cunningham was 20-of-30 for 264 yards. Twice after Green Bay pulled within six points – once in the second quarter and once in the fourth – Cunningham drove Minnesota for TDs, the second on a 49-yard pass to Moss with 3:17 left that put the game away.

AP/Tom Olmscheid

	1	2	3	4	F
Green Bay Packers	0	7	0	7	14
Minnesota Vikings	10	10	0	8	28

First Quarter

Minnesota–(3:03) Gary Anderson 35-yard FG

Minnesota–(13:37) Jimmy Hitchcock 58-yard interception return for TD (Gary Anderson kick)

Second Quarter

Minnesota–(5:23) Gary Anderson 29-yard FG

Green Bay–(11:22) Tyrone Davis 12-yard TD pass from Brett Favre (Ryan Longwell kick)

Minnesota–(14:36) Cris Carter 4-yard TD pass from Randall Cunningham (Gary Anderson kick)

Fourth Quarter

Green Bay–(7:29) Tyrone Davis 2-yard TD pass from Brett Favre (Ryan Longwell kick)

Minnesota–(11:43) Randy Moss 49-yard TD pass from Randall Cunningham (Randall Cunningham 2-point conversion run)

	Packers	Vikings
First Downs	22	15
Rushing	3	4
Passing	19	10
Penalty	0	1
Rushes-Yards	18-53	21-92
Average Per Rush	2.9	4.4
Comp-Att-Int	31-39-1	20-30-1
Net Passing Yards	277	248
Sacks-Yards Lost	3-26	2-16
Average Per Pass Play	6.6	7.8
Return Yards	36	58
Int Ret-Yds	1-15	1-58
Punt Ret-Yds	2-21	0-0
Kick Return Yards	1-17	2-47
Punts-Average	4-44.8	3-54.3
Fumbles-Lost	3-2	0-0
Penalties-Yards	9-48	7-50
Time of Possession	32:11	27:49

RUSHING

GREEN BAY: Holmes 16-51, Favre 2-2.

MINNESOTA: Hoard 3-39, Smith 13-27, Cunningham 4-20, Palmer 1-6.

PASSING

GREEN BAY: Favre 31-39-1-303.

MINNESOTA: Cunningham 20-30-1-264.

RECEIVING

GREEN BAY: Schroeder 7-93, Holmes 5-50, Henderson 5-23, Chmura 4-37, Freeman 3-46, Davis 3-19, Brooks 2-19, Preston 1-13, Blair 1-3.

MINNESOTA: Moss 8-153, Glover 3-38, Carter 3-28, Reed 3-18, Smith 2-10, Tate 1-17.

FUMBLES/LOST

GREEN BAY: Favre 2-1, Henderson 1-1.

MINNESOTA: None.

INTERCEPTIONS

GREEN BAY: Williams 1-15.

MINNESOTA: Hitchcock 1-58.

Attendance: 64,471

AP/Ann Heisenfelt

AP/Ann Heisenfelt

AP/Tom Olmscheid

November 15, 1998 at Minneapolis
Vikings 24, Bengals 3

With its offense struggling for much of the game, Minnesota's defense took over, proving that the Vikings' best season in years is about a lot more than talented receivers and a high-scoring offense.

Dwayne Rudd's 63-yard fumble return late in the third quarter awoke the Vikings and sparked a 24-3 victory over the Cincinnati Bengals. Rudd's score gave the Vikings (9-1) a 14-3 lead. The defense allowed just four first downs the rest of the way.

Randall Cunningham showed no signs of last week's knee surgery, running for a TD and throwing for another, but the Vikings' defense made the biggest plays of the game.

Robert Smith had only 58 yards and Leroy Hoard 52, as it was the first time in seven games an opposing back failed to top 100 against Cincinnati.

David Palmer's 19-yard punt return helped set up Anderson's 32-yard field goal to make it 17-3. After a Hitchcock interception, the Vikings needed just one play – Cunningham's 61-yard TD pass to Moss – to put the game away.

Off to their best start since 1975, the Vikings protected their two-game lead in the NFC Central and their one-game lead over Atlanta in the race for home-field advantage throughout the NFC playoffs.

AP/Tom Olmscheid

	1	2	3	4	F
Cincinnati Bengals	0	3	0	0	3
Minnesota Vikings	7	0	7	10	24

First Quarter

Minnesota–(8:29) Randall Cunningham 3-yard TD run (Gary Anderson kick)

Second Quarter

Cincinnati–(8:04) Doug Pelfrey 37-yard FG

Third Quarter

Minnesota–(11:21) Dwayne Rudd 63-yard defensive fumble return for TD (Gary Anderson kick)

Fourth Quarter

Minnesota–(2:12) Gary Anderson 32-yard FG
Minnesota–(3:34) Randy Moss 61-yard TD pass from Randall Cunningham (Gary Anderson kick)

	Bengals	Vikings
First Downs	15	16
Rushing	7	8
Passing	4	8
Penalty	4	0
Rushes-Yards	34-103	29-125
Average Per Rush	3.0	4.3
Comp-Att-Int	16-27-1	14-22-3
Net Passing Yards	91	224
Sacks-Yards Lost	4-22	2-12
Average Per Pass Play	2.9	9.3
Return Yards	83	61
Int Ret-Yds	3-53	1-34
Punt Ret-Yds	2-30	2-27
Kick Return Yards	1-35	2-56
Punts-Average	5-40.0	4-55.8
Fumbles-Lost	1-1	0-0
Penalties-Yards	2-10	11-105
Time of Possession	32:22	27:38

RUSHING

CINCINNATI: Dillon 21-66, Bennett 7-22, Blake 2-9, Bieniemy 2-7, Pickens 1-0, O'Donnell 1-(-1).
MINNESOTA: Smith 18-58, Hoard 7-52, Cunningham 2-13, Palmer 1-4, Fiedler 1--2.

PASSING

CINCINNATI: O'Donnell 10-17-0-77, Blake 6-10-1-36.
MINNESOTA: Cunningham 13-20-2-224, Fiedler 1-2-1-12.

RECEIVING

CINCINNATI: Scott 4-31, Milne 3-29, Dillon 3-14, Bieniemy 2-16, Pickens 1-8, Battaglia 1-7, Gibson 1-5, Bennett 1-3.
MINNESOTA: Carter 5-87, Moss 4-99, Reed 2-21, Smith 1-10, Evans 1-10, Glover 1-9.

FUMBLES/LOST

CINCINNATI: O'Donnell 1-1.
MINNESOTA: None.

INTERCEPTIONS

CINCINNATI: Hawkins 2-21, Shade 1-32.
MINNESOTA: Hitchcock 1-34.

Attendance: 64,232

AP/Jim Mone

AP/Ann Heisenfelt

AP/Ann Heisenfelt

November 8, 1998 at Minneapolis
Vikings 31, Saints 24

Coming off the bench when Randall Cunningham injured his right ankle and knee early in the game, Brad Johnson led the Vikings to 17 straight points but threw two costly interceptions in Minnesota's 31-24 victory over the New Orleans Saints.

Johnson broke his thumb on his throwing hand on the first play of the third quarter but played the entire half. Sammy Knight got both interceptions and returned the second one 91 yards to tie the score at 24 with 10:10 remaining. After Knight's touchdown, Johnson led the Vikings to the winning score, Leroy Hoard's second short touchdown run of the day, with 3:43 left.

After a 61-yard touchdown run by Robert Smith, the Saints closed to 24-17 on a 9-yard catch by Aaron Craver in the third quarter.

Johnson, who broke a bone in his right leg in Week 2, finished 28-for-38 for 316 yards with one touchdown and the two interceptions.

Gary Anderson made it 10-0 with a 28-yard field goal 1:37 before halftime. Harold Morrow forced and recovered a fumble at the 4 to set up Hoard's first touchdown and a 17-0 lead.

AP/Paul Battaglia

	1	2	3	4	F
New Orleans Saints	0	7	10	7	24
Minnesota Vikings	7	10	7	7	31

First Quarter

Minnesota–(12:28) Cris Carter 14-yard TD pass from Brad Johnson (Gary Anderson kick)

Second Quarter

Minnesota–(13:23) Gary Anderson 28-yard FG

Minnesota–(13:35) Leroy Hoard 4-yard TD run (Gary Anderson kick)

New Orleans–(13:49) Aaron Craver 100-yard kickoff return for TD (Doug Brien kick)

Third Quarter

New Orleans–(7:04) Doug Brien 20-yard FG

Minnesota–(7:27) Robert Smith 61-yard TD run (Gary Anderson kick)

New Orleans–(11:52) Aaron Craver 9-yard TD pass from Billy Joe Tolliver (Doug Brien kick)

Fourth Quarter

New Orleans–(4:50) Sammy Knight 91-yard interception return for TD (Doug Brien kick)

Minnesota–(11:17) Leroy Hoard 1-yard TD run (Gary Anderson kick)

	Saints	Vikings
First Downs	11	23
Rushing	5	7
Passing	6	16
Penalty	0	0
Rushes-Yards	21-52	32-162
Average Per Rush	2.5	5.1
Comp-Att-Int	11-16-0	28-40-2
Net Passing Yards	138	303
Sacks-Yards Lost	3-30	2-13
Average Per Pass Play	7.3	7.2
Return Yards	112	8
Int Ret-Yds	2-98	0-0
Punt Ret-Yds	2-14	1-8
Kick Return Yards	3-135	5-85
Punts-Average	4-42.5	3-45.3
Fumbles-Lost	1-1	0-0
Penalties-Yards	9-50	6-45
Time of Possession	22:51	37:09

RUSHING

NEW ORLEANS: Smith 11-21, Zellars 6-17, Tolliver 3-7, Craver 1-7.
MINNESOTA: Smith 20-137, Hoard 4-11, Evans 3-9, Palmer 1-4, Johnson 4-1.

PASSING

NEW ORLEANS: Tolliver 11-16-0-168.
MINNESOTA: Johnson 28-38-2-316, Cunningham 0-2-0-0.

RECEIVING

NEW ORLEANS: Dawkins 3-44, Craver 2-58, Zellars 2-23, Hastings 2-11, Smith 1-18, Poole 1-14.
MINNESOTA: Glover 9-93, Carter 6-71, Reed 5-90, Palmer 3-18, Hoard 1-19, Smith 1-9, Moss 1-6, Evans 1-5, DeLong 1-5.

FUMBLES/LOST

NEW ORLEANS: Craver 1-1.
MINNESOTA: None.

INTERCEPTIONS

NEW ORLEANS: Knight 2-98.
MINNESOTA: None.

Attendance: 63,779

AP/Ann Heisenfelt

AP/Tom Olmscheid

November 1, 1998 at Tampa
Buccaneers 27, Vikings 24

The Bucs broke out of an offensive funk with a team-record 246 yards rushing and beat the Vikings, who were the NFC's last unbeaten team, 27-24 on Mike Alstott's 6-yard touchdown run with 5:48 to go.

Alstott ran for a career-high 128 yards on 19 carries and Warrick Dunn gained 115 on 18 attempts.

Randall Cunningham was outstanding for Minnesota (7-1), completing 21 of 25 passes for 291 yards and two touchdowns. But his only interception led to a second-

half field goal, and the Vikings' last three possessions didn't produce points.

Cunningham threw TD passes of 44 and 1 yards to Jake Reed, while Robert Smith scored on a 9-yard run and Gary Anderson kicked a 44-yard field goal for Minnesota that made it 17-17 at the half.

The Vikings scored on their fourth straight possession, taking a 24-17 lead on Cunningham's second TD pass to Reed just over five minutes into the third quarter.

AP/Chris O'Meara

	1	2	3	4	F
Minnesota Vikings	7	10	7	0	24
Tampa Bay Buccaneers	7	10	0	10	27

First Quarter
Tampa Bay–(7:15) Warrick Dunn 10-yard TD run (Michael Husted kick)

Minnesota–(11:59) Robert Smith 9-yard TD run (Gary Anderson kick)

Second Quarter
Tampa Bay–(4:13) Reidel Anthony 12-yard TD pass from Trent Dilfer (Michael Husted kick)

Minnesota–(10:44) Jake Reed 44-yard TD pass from Randall Cunningham (Gary Anderson kick)

Tampa Bay–(14:24) Michael Husted 29-yard FG

Minnesota–(15:00) Gary Anderson 44-yard FG

Third Quarter
Minnesota–(5:37) Jake Reed 1-yard TD pass from Randall Cunningham (Gary Anderson kick)

Fourth Quarter
Tampa Bay–(3:13) Michael Husted 38-yard FG

Tampa Bay–(9:12) Mike Alstott 6-yard TD run (Michael Husted kick)

	Vikings	Buccaneers
First Downs	18	22
Rushing	5	11
Passing	12	9
Penalty	1	2
Rushes-Yards	19-70	41-246
Average Per Rush	3.7	6.0
Comp-Att-Int	21-25-1	11-22-0
Net Passing Yards	270	132
Sacks-Yards Lost	2-21	0-0
Average Per Pass Play	10.0	6.0
Return Yards	0	35
Int Ret-Yds	0-0	1-25
Punt Ret-Yds	0-0	2-10
Kick Return Yards	5-96	2-79
Punts-Average	2-42.5	0-0.0
Fumbles-Lost	0-0	0-0
Penalties-Yards	7-66	4-35
Time of Possession	26:25	33:35

RUSHING
MINNESOTA: Smith 13-46, Cunningham 4-15, Evans 1-7, Hoard 1-2.

TAMPA BAY: Alstott 19-128, Dunn 18-115, Anthony 1-2, Dilfer 3-1.

PASSING
MINNESOTA: Cunningham 21-25-1-291.

TAMPA BAY: Dilfer 11-22-0-132.

RECEIVING
MINNESOTA: Reed 6-117, Smith 5-28, Glover 2-55, Moss 2-52, Carter 2-13, Palmer 1-8, Goodwin 1-7, DeLong 1-6, Hoard 1-5.

TAMPA BAY: Anthony 5-65, Dunn 4-49, Emanuel 1-15, Neal 1-3.

INTERCEPTIONS
MINNESOTA: None.

TAMPA BAY: Brooks 1-25.

Attendance: 64,979

AP/Steve Nesius

AP/Scott Audette

Game 7

October 25, 1998 at Detroit
Vikings 34, Lions 13

Randall Cunningham threw two touchdown passes and the Vikings reeled off 17 consecutive points in the third quarter to remain unbeaten with a 34-13 victory over the Lions.

Robert Smith had 134 yards on 19 carries, including a 57-yard touchdown run to ice it for the Vikings (7-0), who defeated Detroit for the second time.

Cunningham was 17-of-30 for 190 yards, including an 11-yard touchdown pass to Jake Reed and a 10-yard scor-

ing toss to Cris Carter. Cunningham, starting his fifth game since Brad Johnson went down with a broken leg, finally showed a little vulnerability, throwing his first two interceptions.

Gary Anderson kicked field goals of 35 and 44 yards for the Vikings.

Jason Hanson kicked field goals of 47 and 48 yards, and Barry Sanders gained 127 yards on 24 carries for the Lions.

AP/Duane Burleson

	1	2	3	4	F
Minnesota Vikings	0	10	17	7	34
Detroit Lions	3	10	0	0	13

First Quarter
Detroit—(12:29) Jason Hanson 47-yard FG

Second Quarter
Minnesota—(3:10) Jake Reed 11-yard TD pass from Randall Cunningham (Gary Anderson kick)
Detroit—(10:45) Johnnie Morton 1-yard TD pass from Charlie Batch (Jason Hanson kick)
Minnesota—(13:44) Gary Anderson 35-yard FG
Detroit—(15:00) Jason Hanson 48-yard FG

Third Quarter
Minnesota—(7:45) Gary Anderson 44-yard FG
Minnesota—(10:18) Cris Carter 10-yard TD pass from Randall Cunningham (Gary Anderson kick)
Minnesota—(13:22) Robert Smith 57-yard TD run (Gary Anderson kick)

Fourth Quarter
Minnesota—(10:52) Jimmy Hitchcock 79-yard interception return for TD (Gary Anderson kick)

	Vikings	Lions
First Downs	23	17
Rushing	6	5
Passing	13	11
Penalty	4	1
Rushes-Yards	27-159	28-137
Average Per Rush	5.9	4.9
Comp-Att-Int	17-30-2	20-37-1
Net Passing Yards	170	214
Sacks-Yards Lost	4-20	4-17
Average Per Pass Play	5.0	5.2
Return Yards	105	0
Int Ret-Yds	1-79	2-0
Punt Ret-Yds	5-26	0-0
Kick Return Yards	2-70	4-85
Punts-Average	2-49.0	8-45.0
Fumbles-Lost	1-1	0-0
Penalties-Yards	7-55	14-169
Time of Possession	27:00	33:00

RUSHING
MINNESOTA: Smith 19-134, Hoard 6-23, Cunningham 1-4, Fiedler 1-2.
DETROIT: Sanders 24-127, Batch 2-8, Rivers 1-2, Vardell 1-0.
PASSING
MINNESOTA: Cunningham 17-30-2-190.
DETROIT: Batch 20-37-1-231.
RECEIVING
MINNESOTA: Carter 5-73, Palmer 4-50, Reed 4-38, Moss 2-14, Glover 1-11, Hoard 1-4.
DETROIT: Morton 7-89, Sanders 6-51, Moore 4-42, Sloan 2-40, Vardell 1-9.
FUMBLES/LOST
MINNESOTA: Smith 1-1.
DETROIT: None.
INTERCEPTIONS
MINNESOTA: Hitchcock 1-79.
DETROIT: Carrier 1-0, Westbrook 1-0.

Attendance: 77,885

AP/Duane Burleson

AP/Carlos Osorio

October 18, 1998 at Minneapolis
Vikings 41, Redskins 7

After a bye week and a chance to relish their big victory at Green Bay, the unbeaten Vikings avoided a letdown with an emphatic 41-7 victory against the Washington Redskins.

Randall Cunningham threw two touchdown passes and Leroy Hoard ran for two as the Vikings scored 41 consecutive points for a 41-7 triumph. The Vikings also had a dominating defensive performance that included five sacks. Robert Smith ran for 103 yards and a touchdown.

Cunningham threw an 11-yard TD pass to Andrew Glover, then Hoard made it 14-7 Vikings with a 1-yard run later in the first quarter.

Moss caught three passes for 50 yards on the final scoring drive of the first half, which Cunningham finished with a 1-yard pass to Cris Carter to make it 21-7 with 14 seconds left in the half. Cunningham finished 20-for-34 for 259 yards and the two TDs. He now has 12 TDs and no interceptions in four-plus games in relief of injured starter Brad Johnson.

Carter had five catches for 109 yards as the Vikings opened a two-game lead over the Packers in the NFC Central.

AP/Ann Heisenfelt

	1	2	3	4	F
Washington Redskins	7	0	0	0	7
Minnesota Vikings	14	7	3	17	41

First Quarter
Washington–Terry Allen 2-yard TD run (Cary Blanchard kick)
Minnesota–Andrew Glover 11-yard TD pass from Randall Cunningham (Gary Anderson kick)
Minnesota–Leroy Hoard 1-yard TD run (Gary Anderson kick)

Second Quarter
Minnesota–Cris Carter 1-yard TD pass from Randall Cunningham (Gary Anderson kick)

Third Quarter
Minnesota–Gary Anderson 49-yard FG

Fourth Quarter
Minnesota–Robert Smith 19-yard TD run (Gary Anderson kick)
Minnesota–Gary Anderson 46-yard FG
Minnesota–Leroy Hoard 1-yard TD run (Gary Anderson kick)

	Redskins	Vikings
First Downs	9	25
Rushing	5	9
Passing	4	15
Penalty	0	1
Rushes-yards	22-82	38-147
Average Per Rush	3.7	3.9
Comp-Att-Int	10-26-1	22-38-0
Net Passing Yards	95	288
Sacks-Yards Lost	5-22	0-0
Average Per Pass Play	3.1	7.6
Interception Return Yards	0-0	1-0
Punt Return Yards	2-35	2-14
Kick Return Yards	3-69	2-42
Punts-Average	8-43.8	5-42.0
Fumbles-Lost	1-0	2-1
Penalties-Yards	11-94	4-35
Time of Possession	26:47	33:13

RUSHING
WASHINGTON: Allen 13-62, Mitchell 2-27, Hicks 5-4, Frerotte 1-1, Matt Turk 1-minus 12.
MINNESOTA: Smith 24-103, Hoard 10-24, Evans 2-10, Cunningham 1-6, Palmer 1-4.
PASSING
WASHINGTON: Frerotte 10-26-1-117.
MINNESOTA: Cunningham 20-34-0-259, Fiedler 2-4-0-29.
RECEIVING
WASHINGTON: Mitchell 3-22, Westbrook 2-35, Connell 1-22, Allen 1-15, Asher 1-9, Davis 1-8, Alexander 1-6.
MINNESOTA: Carter 5-109, Moss 5-64, Smith 4-23, Glover 2-24, Evans 2-9, Hoard 2-7, Palmer 1-33, Reed 1-19.
FUMBLES/LOST
WASHINGTON: Turk.
MINNESOTA: Moss, Hoard.
INTERCEPTIONS
MINNESOTA: Fuller 1-0.

Attendance: 64,004

AP/Tom Olmscheid

AP/Tom Olmscheid

Game 5

October 5, 1998 at Green Bay
Vikings 37, Packers 24

On Monday night in Green Bay, the Vikings silenced the Cheeseheads, as Randall Cunningham and Randy Moss led the Vikings on national television, beating Green Bay 37-24 to establish Minnesota (5-0) as the NFC team to beat.

Cunningham threw for 442 yards – the most ever against the Packers, surpassing the 411 by San Francisco's Joe Montana in 1990. Cunningham was 20-of-32 passing with four touchdowns, no interceptions and no sacks.

Moss had five catches for 190 yards and two touchdowns, plus a 75-yard scoring play negated by a holding penalty.

Minnesota's offense not only demolished the NFL's No. 1 defense, but the Vikings' defense forced Brett Favre to the bench in the fourth quarter with only 114 passing yards, no touchdowns and three interceptions.

The Vikings rolled to a 37-10 lead in the fourth quarter after Moss leaped over two Packers defenders to make a tough catch for a 44-yard touchdown.

AP/Mike Roemer

	1	2	3	4	F
Minnesota Vikings	3	21	3	10	**37**
Green Bay Packers	0	10	0	14	**24**

First Quarter
Minnesota—(11:46) Gary Anderson 33-yard FG

Second Quarter
Green Bay—(0:07) Ryan Longwell 40-yard FG
Minnesota—(2:51) Jake Reed 56-yard TD pass from Randall Cunningham (Gary Anderson kick)
Green Bay—(3:08) Roell Preston 101-yard kickoff return for TD (Ryan Longwell kick)
Minnesota—(5:04) Randy Moss 52-yard TD pass from Randall Cunningham (Gary Anderson kick)
Minnesota—(10:17) Robert Smith 24-yard TD pass from Randall Cunningham (Gary Anderson kick)

Third Quarter
Minnesota—(3:43) Gary Anderson 25-yard FG

Fourth Quarter
Minnesota—(1:29) Gary Anderson 19-yard FG
Minnesota—(4:44) Randy Moss 44-yard TD pass from Randall Cunningham (Gary Anderson kick)
Green Bay—(11:57) Tyrone Davis 11-yard TD pass from Doug Pederson (Ryan Longwell kick)
Green Bay—(14:15) Bill Schroeder 16-yard TD pass from Doug Pederson (Ryan Longwell kick)

	Vikings	Packers
First Downs	22	21
Rushing	3	9
Passing	17	10
Penalty	2	2
Rushes-Yards	34-103	20-102
Average Per Rush	3.0	5.1
Comp-Att-Int	20-32-0	23-39-3
Net Passing Yards	442	204
Sacks-Yards Lost	0-0	2-13
Average Per Pass Play	13.8	5.0
Return Yards	27	9
Int Ret-Yds	3-27	0-0
Punt Ret-Yds	0-0	1-9
Kick Return Yards	2-55	8-256
Punts-Average	1-51.0	3-44.7
Fumbles-Lost	1-1	1-0
Penalties-Yards	8-76	3-20
Time of Possession	**34:23**	**25:37**

RUSHING
MINNESOTA: Smith 25-78, Hoard 3-13, Palmer 2-12, Evans 1-2, Cunningham 2-1, Carter 1--1.
GREEN BAY: Jervey 8-55, Harris 7-27, Henderson 4-10, Freeman 1-10.
PASSING
MINNESOTA: Cunningham 20-32-0-442.
GREEN BAY: Favre 13-23-3-114, Pederson 10-16-0-103.
RECEIVING
MINNESOTA: Carter 8-119, Moss 5-190, Reed 4-89, Smith 2-38, Glover 1-6.
GREEN BAY: Henderson 4-26, Freeman 3-53, Schroeder 3-32, Davis 3-23, Jervey 3-13, Brooks 2-29, Chmura 2-18, Harris 2-12, Mayes 1-11.
FUMBLES/LOST
MINNESOTA: Cunningham 1-1. **GREEN BAY:** Harris 1-0.
INTERCEPTIONS
MINNESOTA: Griffith 2-0, Thomas 1-27.
GREEN BAY: None.

Attendance: 59,849

AP/Garry Dineen

AP/Tom Olmscheid

Game 4

September 27, 1998 at Chicago
Vikings 31, Bears 28

Cornerback Corey Fuller intercepted a sure touchdown, and Randy Moss and Cris Carter had TD receptions in the second half as the Vikings rallied for a 31-28 victory over the Chicago Bears.

With the scores, Moss and Carter have four TD receptions each this year.

Both Minnesota's Randall Cunningham and Chicago's Erik Kramer had four TD passes. Cunningham finished 16-of-25 for 275 yards. Kramer was 25-of-29 for 372 yards.

Cunningham connected with Andrew Glover for a 19-yard score, cutting Chicago's lead to 21-17. Chicago held the 21-17 lead when Kramer moved the Bears to the

Minnesota 10 and had a wide-open Fabien Bownes in the right corner of the end zone. But Fuller ran in front of Bownes just as he was about to catch the ball and tipped it away. Fuller bobbled the ball several times before finally controlling it at the 6 and returning it to the 32.

After Jake Reed caught a 10-yard pass at the Chicago 35, Cunningham double-pumped under heavy pressure, then heaved a pass to the right corner of the end zone. It fell right into Carter's hands to make it 24-21.

Moss caught a 44-yard TD to give Minnesota a 31-21 lead with 10:13 left.

AP/Frank Polich

	1	2	3	4	F
Minnesota Vikings	7	3	14	7	31
Chicago Bears	7	14	0	7	28

First Quarter

Minnesota–(2:17) Robert Smith 67-yard TD pass from Randall Cunningham (Gary Anderson kick)

Chicago–(5:56) Bobby Engram 33-yard TD pass from Erik Kramer (Jeff Jaeger kick)

Second Quarter

Minnesota–(6:22) Gary Anderson 50-yard FG

Chicago–(8:48) Chris Penn 23-yard TD pass from Erik Kramer (Jeff Jaeger kick)

Chicago–(14:32) Bobby Engram 4-yard TD pass from Erik Kramer (Jeff Jaeger kick)

Third Quarter

Minnesota–(3:36) Andrew Glover 19-yard TD pass from Randall Cunningham (Gary Anderson kick)

Minnesota–(13:16) Cris Carter 35-yard TD pass from Randall Cunningham (Gary Anderson kick)

Fourth Quarter

Minnesota–(4:54) Randy Moss 44-yard TD pass from Randall Cunningham (Gary Anderson kick)

Chicago–(13:07) Ryan Wetnight 19-yard TD pass from Erik Kramer (Jeff Jaeger kick)

	Vikings	Bears
First Downs	17	23
Rushing	5	5
Passing	10	16
Penalty	2	2
Rushes-Yards	27-93	26-91
Average Per Rush	3.4	3.5
Comp-Att-Int	16-25-0	25-39-1
Net Passing Yards	258	361
Sacks-Yards Lost	3-17	1-11
Average Per Pass Play	9.2	9.0
Return Yards	79	15
Int Ret-Yds	1-26	0-0
Punt Ret-Yds	1-53	1-15
Kick Return Yards	3-73	5-75
Punts-Average	5-35.4	6-41.7
Fumbles-Lost	0-0	0-0
Penalties-Yards	4-38	9-55
Time of Possession	26:57	33:03

RUSHING
MINNESOTA: Smith 19-76, Hoard 2-7, Cunningham 5-6, Moss 1-4.
CHICAGO: Bennett 11-47, Enis 14-43, Hallock 1-1.

PASSING
MINNESOTA: Cunningham 16-25-0-275.
CHICAGO: Kramer 25-39-1-372.

RECEIVING
MINNESOTA: Carter 4-68, Reed 3-22, Smith 2-83, Moss 2-52, Glover 2-33, Palmer 1-14, Evans 1-6, Cunningham 1-3.
CHICAGO: Engram 6-123, Penn 4-73, Hallock 4-42, Bownes 3-56, Wetnight 3-36, Mayes 2-17, Bennett 2-16, Chancey 1-9.

INTERCEPTIONS
MINNESOTA: Fuller 1-26.
CHICAGO: None.

Attendance: 57,783

AP/Frank Polich

AP/Frank Polich

AP/Frank Polich

September 20, 1998 at Minneapolis
Vikings 29, Lions 6

The Vikings held Barry Sanders to 12 yards on 13 carries after halftime and forced three turnovers to pull away for a 29-6 victory.

Gary Anderson kicked five field goals for the Vikings, whose offense struggled in the red zone with Randall Cunningham replacing injured Brad Johnson at quarterback. Still, Cunningham threw a 5-yard touchdown pass to Randy Moss in the third quarter after a 44-yard punt return by David Palmer, and Leroy Hoard scored on an 11-yard run early in the fourth quarter after Detroit fumbled deep in its own end. Cunningham was 20-for-35 for 220 yards.

The Vikings tied it at halftime on two short Anderson field goals. Moss beat double coverage in the back of the end zone and grabbed the tiebreaking TD pass over the head of safety Mark Carrier.

Anderson's third field goal made it 16-6 Vikings, and when McDaniel forced and recovered a fumble on Detroit's next possession, Anderson kicked his fourth field goal with 1:02 left in the third.

The Vikings had five sacks, including 1.5 by John Randle.

AP/Jim Mone

	1	2	3	4	F
Detroit Lions	3	3	0	0	6
Minnesota Vikings	0	6	13	10	29

First Quarter
Detroit–(10:59) Jason Hanson 37-yard FG

Second Quarter
Detroit–(2:09) Jason Hanson 49-yard FG
Minnesota–(8:36) Gary Anderson 27-yard FG
Minnesota–(13:09) Gary Anderson 28-yard FG

Third Quarter
Minnesota–(3:19) Randy Moss 5-yard TD pass from Randall Cunningham (Gary Anderson kick)
Minnesota–(11:24) Gary Anderson 42-yard FG
Minnesota–(13:58) Gary Anderson 29-yard FG

Fourth Quarter
Minnesota–(0:15) Leroy Hoard 11-yard TD run (Gary Anderson kick)
Minnesota–(13:09) Gary Anderson 34-yard FG

	Lions	Vikings
First Downs	19	17
Rushing	8	3
Passing	10	13
Penalty	1	1
Rushes-Yards	31-137	24- 76
Average Per Rush	4.4	3.2
Comp-Att-Int	20-40-2	20-35-0
Net Passing Yards	142	211
Sacks-Yards Lost	5-18	2-9
Average Per Pass Play	3.2	5.7
Return Yards	1	60
Int Ret-Yds	0-0	2-0
Punt Ret-Yds	1-1	3-60
Kick Return Yards	6-123	3- 62
Punts-Average	4-43.0	4-47.0
Fumbles-Lost	2-2	2-0
Penalties-Yards	9-69	5-45
Time of Possession	34:15	25:45

RUSHING
DETROIT: Sanders 22-69, Batch 8-63, Rivers 1-5.
MINNESOTA: Smith 15-39, Hoard 5-16, Palmer 1-15, Cunningham 3-6.
PASSING
DETROIT: Batch 20-40-2-160.
MINNESOTA: Cunningham 20-35-0-220.
RECEIVING
DETROIT: Moore 9-66, Morton 5-57, Sanders 5-29, Chryplewicz 1-8.
MINNESOTA: Moss 5-37, Glover 3-50, Reed 3-44, Carter 3-27, DeLong 2-28, Smith 2-10, Palmer 1-18, Hoard 1-6.
FUMBLES/LOST
DETROIT: Batch 1-1, Chryplewicz 1-1.
MINNESOTA: Palmer 1-0, Moss 1-0.
INTERCEPTIONS
DETROIT: None.
MINNESOTA: Griffith 1-0, Fuller 1-0.

Attendance: 63,107

AP/Tom Olmscheid

AP/Tom Olmscheid

September 13, 1998 at St. Louis
Vikings 38, Rams 31

The Vikings scored five touchdowns but still needed a defensive stop on the final play to clinch a 38-31 victory over the St. Louis Rams.

Rams quarterback Tony Banks scrambled for an 8-yard gain but was stopped less than a yard away from the end zone as time expired.

Randall Cunningham subbed for injured Brad Johnson and threw a 19-yard touchdown pass to Cris Carter with 2:09 left for the winning score. Robert Smith rushed for a career-high 179 yards and two first-half TDs, including a 74-yard score for the Vikings, who led 24-10 at halftime before trading points with the Rams the rest of the way.

Banks connected with Isaac Bruce on an 80-yard TD that tied the score 31-31 early in the fourth quarter. Banks also threw a career-high four interceptions.

Johnson was 18-for-31 for 208 yards and one touchdown, two interceptions and one costly fumble before he sprained his right ankle after the Rams tied it at 31-31. On the winning play, Cunningham gunned the ball in the right corner of the end zone to Carter. The catch was the 765th of Carter's career as he passed James Lofton for sixth place on the NFL career list. Vikings rookie Randy Moss had six catches for 89 yards.

AP/James A. Finley

	1	2	3	4	F
Minnesota Vikings	14	10	7	7	38
St. Louis Rams	0	10	14	7	31

First Quarter

Minnesota–(4:50) Robert Smith 24-yard TD run (Gary Anderson kick)

Minnesota–(11:20) Andrew Glover 3-yard TD pass from Brad Johnson (Gary Anderson kick)

Second Quarter

St. Louis–(0:05) Greg Hill 1-yard TD run (Jeff Wilkins kick)

Minnesota–(10:42) Gary Anderson 24-yard FG

St. Louis–(12:36) Jeff Wilkins 53-yard FG

Minnesota–(13:11) Robert Smith 74-yard TD run (Gary Anderson kick)

Third Quarter

St. Louis–(9:45) Greg Hill 5-yard TD run (Jeff Wilkins kick)

St. Louis–(11:23) Eddie Kennison 71-yard punt return for TD (Jeff Wilkins kick)

Minnesota–(14:14) Leroy Hoard 1-yard TD run (Gary Anderson kick)

Fourth Quarter

St. Louis–(0:10) Isaac Bruce 80-yard TD pass from Tony Banks (Jeff Wilkins kick)

Minnesota–(12:51) Cris Carter 19-yard TD pass from Randall Cunningham (Gary Anderson kick)

	Vikings	Rams
First Downs	23	22
Rushing	7	9
Passing	14	11
Penalty	2	2
Rushes-Yards	31-194	27-135
Average Per Rush	6.3	5.0
Comp-Att-Int	21-37-2	25-45-4
Net Passing Yards	227	275
Sacks-Yards Lost	3-22	1-8
Average Per Pass Play	5.7	6.0
Return Yards	71	89
Int Ret-Yds	4 39	2-0
Punt Ret-Yds	2-32	3-89
Kick Return Yards	4-89	5-98
Punts-Average	5-40.8	5-31.0
Fumbles-Lost	1-1	0-0
Penalties-Yards	10-81	9-85
Time of Possession	30:18	29:42

RUSHING

MINNESOTA: Smith 23-179, Johnson 4-8, Hoard 2-4, Evans 2-3.

ST. LOUIS: Hill 21-82, Bruce 1-30, Banks 4-24, Lee 1--1.

PASSING

MINNESOTA: Johnson 18-31-2-208, Cunningham 3-6-0-41.

ST. LOUIS: Banks 25-45-4-283.

RECEIVING

MINNESOTA: Moss 6-89, Carter 4-60, Glover 3-37, Smith 3-7, Hoard 2-22, Reed 2-13, Walsh 1-21.

ST. LOUIS: Bruce 11-192, Conwell 5-28, Lee 5-24, Thomas 1-18, Kennison 1-9, Hill 1-6, Harris 1-6.

FUMBLES/LOST

MINNESOTA: Johnson 1-1.

ST. LOUIS: None.

INTERCEPTIONS

MINNESOTA: Griffith 2-25, Gray 1-11, Hitchcock 1-3.

ST. LOUIS: Jones 1-0, Lyght 1-0.

Attendance: 56,234

AP/James A. Finley

AP/Mary Butkus

AP/James A. Finley

Game 1

September 6, 1998 at Minneapolis
Vikings 31, Bucs 7

Randy Moss caught two long touchdown passes to lead the Vikings to an easy 31-7 victory over Tampa Bay in the season opener. Cris Carter also had two touchdown receptions, and Brad Johnson tied a career high with four touchdown passes.

Moss blew the game open with a 48-yard touchdown and then a 31-yarder on consecutive possessions as Minnesota took a 21-0 first-half lead.

Tampa Bay's running game generated only 68 yards with Pro Bowl backs Warrick Dunn and Mike Alstott. Alstott fumbled on the second drive of the game, leading to Moss' first touchdown. Tampa missed a field goal on its next drive and Minnesota responded with Moss' second TD.

With the win, the Vikings have won 11 of their last 12 openers. The exception was last year's 28-14 loss to Tampa Bay.

AP/Paul Battaglia

	1	2	3	4	F
Tampa Bay Buccaneers	0	0	7	0	**7**
Minnesota Vikings	14	7	0	10	**31**

First Quarter

Minnesota–(8:29) Cris Carter 1-yard TD pass from Brad Johnson (Gary Anderson kick)

Minnesota–(13:16) Randy Moss 48-yard TD pass from Brad Johnson (Gary Anderson kick)

Second Quarter

Minnesota–(8:46) Randy Moss 31-yard TD pass from Brad Johnson (Gary Anderson kick)

Third Quarter

Tampa Bay–(9:46) Lorenzo Neal 3-yard TD pass from Trent Dilfer (Michael Husted kick)

Fourth Quarter

Minnesota–(0:44) Gary Anderson 43-yard FG

Minnesota–(9:36) Cris Carter 18-yard TD pass from Brad Johnson (Gary Anderson kick)

	`Buccaneers	Vikings
First Downs	17	19
Rushing	4	5
Passing	13	11
Penalty	0	3
Rushes-Yards	23- 68	27-117
Average Per Rush	3.0	4.3
Comp-Att-Int	23-37-1	15-25-1
Net Passing Yards	251	181
Sacks-Yards Lost	1-9	1-8
Average Per Pass Play	6.6	7.0
Return Yards	45	45
Int Ret-Yds	1-22	1-38
Punt Ret-Yds	2-23	2-7
Kick Return Yards	5-130	2-31
Punts-Average	4-41.0	4- 42.5
Fumbles-Lost	1- 1	0- 0
Penalties-Yards	12-124	4- 30
Time of Possession	**33:30**	**26:30**

RUSHING

TAMPA BAY: Dunn 12-47, Alstott 7-12, Ellison 3-6, Dilfer 1-3.
MINNESOTA: Smith 18-90, Hoard 7-29, Johnson 2-2.

PASSING

TAMPA BAY: Dilfer 17-25-0-207, Walsh 6-12-1-53.
MINNESOTA: Johnson 15-25-1-189.

RECEIVING

TAMPA BAY: Emanuel 7-98, Anthony 4-58, Alstott 4-29, Williams 2-24, Dunn 2-21, Hape 2-11, Moore 1-16, Neal 1-3.
MINNESOTA: Carter 5-31, Moss 4-95, Smith 2-23, Hoard 2-23, Evans 1-14, Reed 1-3.

FUMBLES/LOST

TAMPA BAY: Alstott 1-1.
MINNESOTA: None.

INTERCEPTIONS

TAMPA BAY: Mincy 1-22.
MINNESOTA: Hitchcock 1-38.

Attendance: 62,538

AP/Tom Olmscheid

AP/Tom Olmscheid

AP/Tom Olmscheid

Randy Moss

Vikings' rookie phenom is proving a lot of people wrong

by Roland Lazenby

Allsport/Jamie Squire

Randy Moss' West Virginia homeland is a place of craggy mountains, fetching river valleys and startlingly beautiful spreads of bluegrass, all highlighted by the noxious fumes of chemical plants.

The name of his high school speaks volumes. DuPont.

In all fairness, the chemical plants are less of an imposing presence these days in the Charleston area, where Moss grew up. But the region will be long in shedding the decades of pollution from those plants. Some say it's ingrained in the regional character, the reason that John Denver had to describe the place as "almost heaven" instead of, say, just plain heaven.

Anyway, by nature West Virginians are a people comfortable with the duality of things. And that's why they seem to be entirely comfortable with the duality of Randy Moss, the good and the bad.

Like his homeland, Moss seems to have both in abundance. Instead of rustic beauty, Moss has a rugged athleticism. And then there's the toxic side of his persona.

While most of this toxicity can be written off to youthful indiscretion, it should be noted that Moss has paid dearly for those indiscretions. But that's the way it works sometimes for people with superior talent. They pay for it.

Trading almost exclusively on his abilities, DuPont won two state football championships during his tenure there. In basketball, he was the state's two-time player of the year and had already drawn the rapt attention of NBA scouts. In track, he was a state champion sprinter. In baseball, a major prospect as a center fielder.

Allsport/Jonathan Daniel

But his football was the real deal, evidenced by his signing a grant in aid with Notre Dame in the spring of 1995. Then, in shades of Allen Iverson, Moss was charged criminally and convicted as the result of a fight with a white student at DuPont. With the 30-day jail sentence and suspension from school came notification that Notre Dame no longer needed his services.

Notre Dame coach Lou Holtz did help Moss sign on at Florida State, where he promptly wowed them in scrimmages during a redshirt year. Problem was, Moss didn't quite wow them enough because when he tested positive for marijuana over the summer of 1996, the Seminoles set him free.

The best option for him was back home, to transfer to 1-AA Marshall University, west of Charleston on Interstate 64, where the West Virginia highlands spread out into bluegrass and Moss sprouted into college football's deadliest weapon.

In two brief college seasons, he had 53 touchdown receptions and 3,529 yards gained off caught balls, all the product of his speed, strength, size and leaping ability.

His first season at Marshall he delivered the 1-AA national title for the Thundering Herd. The victim in the championship game was Montana, whose athletic director sent FSU's Bobby Bowden a note afterward lamenting, "If you hadn't kicked Moss off your team, we'd both be national champions."

It wasn't the first time that a key observer had come to the conclusion that Moss could dominate the game at virtually any level. Indeed, Moss himself thrived on that confidence.

After Marshall moved up to 1-A competition the next season and Moss again excelled (he finished fourth in the Heisman voting), he knew it was time to turn professional. He had his heart absolutely set on being a Dallas Cowboy. After all, America's Team clearly needed the game's next great receiver to contin-

Allsport/Tom Hauck

Allsport/Matthew Stockman

ue its reign, and he was the obvious choice.

Unfortunately, that's when his toxicity again intruded upon his happy scene. A fight with girlfriend Libby Offutt, the mother of his two young children, brought domestic battery charges filed against the two of them. They later kissed and made up, but the damage had been done. Pro teams loved his talent but were terrified by his corn rows and the "Superfreak" tattoo.

Moss plummeted in the 1998 draft, all the way to 21st where Vikings coach Dennis Green happily won a debate within the front office over the risk of drafting the talented young receiver from West Virginia.

A deep depression had fallen over Moss on draft day when Green finally phoned and informed him that Minnesota, for whom Moss' half brother, Eric, was an offensive lineman, had selected him. Yes, Moss had lost about $4 million by falling so far in the draft, Green told him. But if he came in and used his vast talent wisely, he'd soon make that up, the coach advised.

Moss took it as a cue. He signed a four-year deal early and was in training camp from the very first minute with a mission to show the 20 teams that passed him up what a tremendous mistake they'd made.

It didn't take long.

By the 13th game of the season, a blowout of the Chicago Bears, Moss had set a new record for receptions by a rookie and was steaming his way toward a Pro Bowl selection.

He scorched the Bears for three touchdown receptions in early December, just days after having done the same thing to the Dallas Cowboys. The three strikes against Chicago gave him 14 TD receptions for the season, with three games left to go. Moss' 14 touchdowns broke the league's rookie record set by Green Bay's Billy Howton in 1952 and matched by San Diego's John Jefferson in 1979.

Allsport/Tom Pidgeon

Allsport/Jonathan Daniel

Far better was the fact that he had helped the Vikings to a 12-1 start, their best since their glory days in the 1970s.

"I'm having a lot of fun," Moss told reporters afterward. "My individual goals I'll look back at when the season is over. Now, I'm trying to do whatever I can to go to the Super Bowl.

"Like I said, I want to come in here and do whatever I can to tear this league apart and right now I think I'm on the verge of doing that and I hope I can continue to do so."

It must be pointed out that by December hardly anyone in the NFL had the slightest question about his character.

Over his brief months in the league, Moss had conducted himself with a borderline gentility. Heck, the guy didn't even dance in the end zone when he scored touchdowns.

He had used his leaping ability to jump into the arms of Vikings fans in the Metrodome on occasion, but that was just to get a few congratulatory pats and hugs from the faithful.

Lord knows Moss has earned them. Just the same, Green and his veteran players kept an eye on the circumstances to make sure that Moss didn't rise too high too quickly for his own good.

"I think it takes a lot of days, consecutive days, making the right decision," Minnesota's Cris Carter said of Moss at the start of the season. "I think if he continues on the path that he is on now, his past will

be behind him before he realizes it. But he has to realize that his past is not a myth. It is not something that the media has created. It is something that he brought upon himself. He realizes that. All he can control is what is going on today and what is going to happen in the future. If he wants people to stop asking him about his past, then he needs to continue to making good decisions on a daily basis."

The blessing, for both Moss and the Vikings, was that he did fall in the draft. The bright lights and party atmosphere of Dallas might well have destroyed the 21-year-old rookie. In Minnesota, he found a roster brimming with strong, veteran leaders such as quarterback Randall Cunningham and Carter. Being drafted by the Vikings "is the best thing that could have ever happened to me," Moss conceded. "If I would have been in the top 10, it would have been a struggle … Here, I'm not in a situation where all the attention is on me."

"I came out of a situation that was very similar to Randy and I know how some people judged me and I didn't want to do that to him," Carter has explained. "So I gave him the benefit of the doubt. The one thing about Randy and I that he understands about me, I tell him that if you can't tell me the truth, I rather you not tell me anything. And that is the basis of our relationship. So, over the course of our relationship there is certain things that I don't talk to him about. When the time is right, he will mention them, and then we will talk about them, but I don't force myself on him; especially as far as social issues are concerned. Only thing I really force on him as far as understanding of the game and concentrating on being informed in the meeting, what it takes to practice, the schedule, Wednesday, Thursday, Friday, those types of things. Because those are the

things that I know that he won't be offended about."

"When I showed up in Mankato for training camp, I got bombarded with questions," Moss said. "You know, am I ready to go? Am I happy to be here? And my first answer was, 'I'm ready to just play.' And, day in and day out, I just want to play well. I think I told Cris I'm going to come in here and try to do the best I can to rip the NFL up."

He began the process with a TD catch in his first exhibition game. Aligned as the third receiver with excellent veterans Jake Reed and Carter, Moss added a new dimension to the Minnesota offense.

In the first game of the regular season he scored twice. In game number two, he put on a blocking display that helped produce three touchdowns. He won the fourth game with a leaping, last-minute reception.

Then he exploded against the Green Bay Packers in Game 5, and the praise washed in like a West Virginia gully gusher.

Against the Cowboys on Thanksgiving Day, Moss caught three TD passes, two for 56 yards and another for 51.

"Randy has that rare ability to make a play no matter whether he's covered or not," Minnesota offensive coordinator Brian Billick said. "You know with him there's always a chance he might pull this thing off and score. He's a little bit like Barry Sanders that way – well, I'd better not say that, because Barry's played so much longer."

"I think we were expecting great things out of him," Cris Carter said. "It's hard to really tell what he's going to do. But we knew – especially with the offense that we have – we knew he'd put up numbers. There are certain things he might do on a certain play that might surprise us. But the overall output? The productivity? We're not surprised."

By the time he was through with the Bears in game 13, he already had better than 1,100 yards and 55 catches.

"The kid is just having a tremendous year," Bears linebacker Rico McDonald said. "He's a tremendous receiver, and you have to give him the credit."

"He is the most natural receiver that I have ever seen without any work or, especially at the early stages of your career," Cris Carter offered. "You have to realize he is only 21 and I don't believe he has been involved with the very sophisticated passing attack (in college). But he is very, very natural as far as his movements to the ball, his route running. He is a tremendous athlete, not only just jumping for the ball, but unbelievably fluid going to the ball, very comfortable in a crowd and very, very tough. Has unbelievable drive inside of him to be a good player."

"You learn from the things you do and the mistakes you make," Randall Cunningham observed. "I'm thankful I've made those mistakes. I hope most of them are in the past. As far as Randy, he's going to make some mistakes. Hopefully, you guys (the media) won't scrutinize him too tough. He's a young kid. We'll do all we can, but he has to be himself."

The circumstances seem just fine for Vikings fans. In fact, they're beginning to understand Moss in terms of where he came from. He's "almost heaven." ∎

1998-99 Statistics

Team Stats

	Minnesota	Opponents
Total First Downs	262	249
Rushing	76	84
Passing	164	144
Penalty	22	21
3rd Down: Made/Att	84/161	62/175
3rd Down Pct.	52.2	35.4
4th Down: Made/Att	2/2	16/29
4th Down Pct.	100.0	55.2
Possession Avg.	28:45	31:15
Total Net Yards	5089	4238
Avg. Per Game	391.5	326.0
Avg. Per Play	6.5	5.1
Net Yards Rushing	1565	1331
Avg. Per Game	120.4	102.4
Avg. Per Attempt	4.4	3.9
Total Rushes	355	339
Net Yards Passing	3524	2907
Avg. Per Game	271.1	223.6
Avg. Per Play	8.25	5.84
Sacked/Yards Lost	22/144	32/207
Gross Yards	3668	3114
Att./Completions	405/252	466/274
Completion Pct.	62.2	58.8
Had Intercepted	14	16
Punts/Average	44/44.2	61/42.4
Penalties/Yards	94/827	108/976
Fumbles/Ball Lost	9/4	13/8
Touchdowns	53	29
Rushing	16	10
Passing	33	15
Misc.	4	4

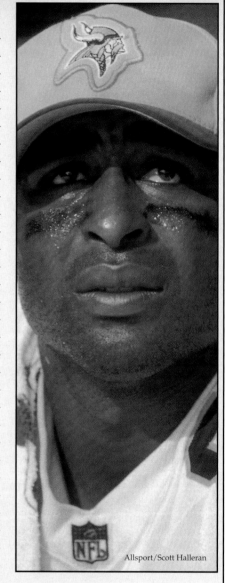

Allsport/Scott Halleran

Scoring

	Total TD	Rush. TD	Rec. TD	FG	PAT	S	Pts.
Gary Anderson	0	0	0	23/23	51/51	0	120
Randy Moss	14	0	14	0/0	0/0	0	86
Leroy Hoard	10	9	1	0/0	0/0	0	60
Cris Carter	9	0	9	0/0	0/0	0	54
Robert Smith	8	6	2	0/0	0/0	0	48
Jake Reed	4	0	4	0/0	0/0	0	24
Andrew Glover	3	0	3	0/0	0/0	0	18
Jimmy Hitchcock	2	0	0	0/0	0/0	0	12
Dwayne Rudd	2	0	0	0/0	0/0	0	12
Randall Cunningham	1	1	0	0/0	0/0	0	8

Scoring

	Total TD	Rush. TD	Rec. TD	FG	PAT	S	Pts.
Vikings	53	16	33	23/23	51/51	0	442
Opponents	25	10	15	15	13/15	0	242

Scoring By Periods

	1	2	3	4	OT	Pts.
Vikings	118	110	100	114	0	442
Opponents	33	80	55	74	0	242

Passing

	Att.	Cmp.	Yds.	Cmp%	Yd./Att.	TD	TD%	INT	INT%	Long	Sack/Lost	Rating
Randall Cunningham	305	188	2914	61.6	9.55	27	8.9	8	0.0	67t	17/112	111.8
Brad Johnson	94	61	713	64.9	7.59	6	6.4	5	0.1	48t	4/30	86.9
Jay Fiedler	6	3	41	50.0	6.83	0	0.0	1	0.2	19	0/0	32.6

Rushing

	No.	Yds.	Avg.	Long	TD
Robert Smith	215	1013	4.7	74t	6
Leroy Hoard	74	347	4.7	50t	9
Randall Cunningham	26	96	3.7	19	1
David Palmer	9	58	6.4	15	0
Chuck Evans	15	47	3.1	12	0
Brad Johnson	10	7	0.7	4	0
Randy Moss	1	4	4.0	4	0
Cris Carter	1	-1	-1.0	-1	0
Jay Fiedler	4	-6	-1.5	-1	0

Receiving

	No.	Yds.	Avg.	Long	TD
Cris Carter	57	821	14.4	54t	9
Randy Moss	55	1120	20.4	61t	14
Jake Reed	34	474	13.9	56t	4
Andrew Glover	30	435	14.5	36	3
Robert Smith	24	241	10.0	67t	2
Leroy Hoard	16	160	10.0	24t	1
David Palmer	12	145	12.1	33	0
Chuck Evans	8	61	7.6	14	0
Greg DeLong	7	54	7.7	17	0
Matt Hatchette	3	26	8.7	11	0
Chris Walsh	2	46	23.0	25	0
Randall Cunningham	1	-3	-3.0	-3	0
Hunter Goodwin	1	7	7.0	7	0
Robert Tate	1	17	17.0	17	0
Moe Williams	1	64	64.0	64	0

Field Goals

	1-19	20-29	30-39	40-49	50+
Gary Anderson	1/1	8/8	6/6	7/7	1/1
Vikings	1/1	8/8	6/6	7/7	1/1
Opponents	0/0	0/0	0/0	0/0	0/0

Allsport/Scott Halleran

1998-99 Statistics

Individual Defense

	Tackles	Solo	Asst.	Sacks	Fumble Rec.
Ed McDaniel	108	77	31	6.0	1
Dwayne Rudd	83	72	11	1.0	3
Robert Griffith	72	59	13	0.0	0
Corey Fuller	68	61	7	0.0	0
Orlando Thomas	59	50	9	0.5	0
Jimmy Hitchcock	54	47	7	0.0	0
Dixon Edwards	45	28	17	0.0	0
Derrick Alexander	36	31	5	6.5	0
John Randle	34	22	12	8.5	1
Tony Williams	30	21	9	1.0	1
Torrian Gray	26	25	1	1.0	1
Jerry Ball	24	17	7	0.0	0
Duane Clemons	23	16	7	2.5	0
Pete Bercich	17	14	3	0.0	0
Kailee Wong	17	15	2	1.5	0
Kivuusama Mays	12	10	2	0.0	0
Stalin Colinet	10	5	5	1.0	0
Bobby Houston	10	7	3	0.0	0
Robert Tate	10	9	1	0.0	0
Duane Butler	9	8	1	0.0	0
Jason Fisk	9	6	3	1.5	0
Ramos McDonald	9	4	5	0.0	0
Chris Walsh	8	7	1	0.0	0
Harold Morrow	6	5	1	0.0	1
Moe Williams	4	4	0	0.0	1
Antonio Banks	3	3	0	0.0	0
Hunter Goodwin	3	3	0	0.0	1
Mitch Berger	2	2	0	0.0	0
Cris Carter	2	2	0	0.0	0
Leroy Hoard	2	2	0	0.0	0
Randall McDaniel	2	2	0	0.0	0
Randy Moss	2	2	0	0.0	0
Jake Reed	2	2	0	0.0	0
Randall Cunningham	1	1	0	0.0	0
Greg DeLong	1	1	0	0.0	0
Mike Morris	1	1	0	0.0	0
Anthony Phillips	1	1	0	0.0	0
Robert Smith	1	1	0	0.0	0
Korey Stringer	1	1	0	0.0	0
Vikings	807	644	163	31.0	10
Opponents	776	588	188	21.0	9

Allsport/Jonathan Daniel

Punting

	No.	Avg.	Net	T'back	In20	Long	Blocked
Mitch Berger	44	44.2	37.3	2	13	66	0
Vikings	44	44.2	37.3	2	13	66	0
Opponents	61	42.4	35.8	7	17	59	0

Kickoff Returns

	No.	Yds.	Avg.	Long	TD
David Palmer	39	867	22.2	44	0
Moe Williams	2	19	9.5	12	0
Robert Tate	1	20	20.0	20	0
Vikings	42	906	21.6	44	0
Opponents	52	1351	26.0	101t	2

Punt Returns

	Ret.	F.Catch	Yds.	Avg.	Long	TD
David Palmer	23	15	268	11.7	53	0
Randy Moss	1	2	0	0.0	0	0
Vikings	24	17	268	11.2	53	0
Opponents	20	11	266	13.3	71t	1

Interceptions

	No.	Yds.	Avg.	Long	TD
Jimmy Hitchcock	6	212	35.3	79t	2
Robert Griffith	5	25	5.0	17	0
Corey Fuller	3	26	8.7	26	0
Torrian Gray	1	11	11.0	11	0
Orlando Thomas	1	27	27.0	27	0
Vikings	16	301	18.8	79t	2
Opponents	14	221	15.8	91t	1

Allsport/Tom Hauck

Allsport/Scott Halleran

Allsport/Scott Halleran

1998-99 Vikings

No.	Name	Position	Height	Weight	Birthdate	Experience	College
90	Alexander, Derrick	DE	6-4	292	11/13/73	4	Florida State
1	Anderson, Gary	K	5-11	176	7/16/59	17	Syracuse
	Ayanbadejo, Obafemi	RB	6-2	230	3/5/75	1	San Diego State
96	Ball, Jerry	DT	6-1	345	12/15/64	12	Southern Methodist
38	Bass, Anthony	DB	6-1	192	3/27/75	R	Bethune-Cookman
56	Bercich, Pete	LB	6-1	247	12/23/71	4	Notre Dame
17	Berger, Mitch	P	6-2	220	6/24/72	3	Colorado
75	Birk, Matt	T	6-4	315	7/23/76	R	Harvard
74	Bobo, Orlando	G	6-3	301	2/9/74	2	Northeast Louisiana
8	Bouman, Todd	QB	6-2	216	8/1/72	1	St. Cloud State
31	Butler, Duane	DB	6-1	211	11/29/73	2	Illinois State
80	Carter, Cris	WR	6-3	220	11/25/65	12	Ohio State
62	Christy, Jeff	C	6-3	280	2/3/69	6	Pittsburgh
92	Clemons, Duane	DE	6-5	274	5/23/74	3	California
99	Colinet, Stalin	DE	6-6	281	7/19/74	2	Boston College
7	Cunningham, Randall	QB	6-4	219	3/27/63	13	Nevada-Las Vegas
32	Darden, Tony	DB	5-11	196	8/11/75	R	Texas Tech
85	DeLong, Greg	TE	6-4	256	4/3/73	4	North Carolina
71	Dixon, David	G	6-5	359	1/5/69	5	Arizona State
59	Edwards, Dixon	LB	6-1	234	3/25/68	8	Michigan State
29	Evans, Chuck	RB	6-1	252	4/16/67	6	Clark Atlanta
11	Fiedler, Jay	QB	6-1	214	12/29/71	3	Dartmouth
72	Fisk, Jason	DT	6-3	296	9/4/72	4	Stanford
27	Fuller, Corey	DB	5-10	217	5/1/71	4	Florida State
82	Glover, Andrew	TE	6-6	257	8/12/67	8	Grambling State
87	Goodwin, Hunter	TE	6-5	271	10/10/72	3	Texas A&M
23	Gray, Torrian	DB	6-0	200	3/18/74	2	Virginia Tech
24	Griffith, Robert	DB	5-11	199	11/30/70	5	San Diego State
89	Hatchette, Matt	WR	6-2	200	5/1/74	2	Langston
37	Hitchcock, Jimmy	DB	5-10	196	11/9/70	4	North Carolina
44	Hoard, Leroy	RB	5-11	225	5/15/68	9	Michigan
55	Houston, Bobby	LB	6-2	242	10/26/67	8	North Carolina State
14	Johnson, Brad	QB	6-5	225	9/13/68	7	Florida State
61	Lindsay, Everett	G	6-4	302	9/18/70	5	Mississippi
76	Liwienski, Chris	T	6-5	304	8/2/75	R	Indiana
53	Mays, Kivuusama	LB	6-3	247	1/7/75	R	North Carolina
58	McDaniel, Ed	LB	5-11	230	2/23/69	7	Clemson
64	McDaniel, Randall	G	6-3	290	12/19/64	11	Arizona State
34	McDonald, Ramos	DB	5-11	195	4/30/76	R	New Mexico
68	Morris, Mike	C	6-5	276	2/22/61	12	Northeast Missouri State
33	Morrow, Harold	RB	5-11	221	2/24/73	3	Auburn
79	Moss, Eric	G	6-4	315	9/25/74	1	Ohio State
84	Moss, Randy	WR	6-4	197	2/13/77	R	Marshall
22	Palmer, David	RB	5-8	173	11/19/72	5	Alabama
28	Phillips, Anthony	DB	6-2	225	10/5/70	4	Texas A&M - Kingsville
93	Randle, John	DE	6-1	294	12/12/67	9	Texas A&M - Kingsville
86	Reed, Jake	WR	6-3	216	9/28/67	8	Grambling State
57	Rudd, Dwayne	LB	6-2	248	2/3/76	2	Alabama
78	Sapp, Bob	G	6-4	319	9/22/73	2	Washington
26	Smith, Robert	RB	6-2	212	3/4/72	6	Ohio State
73	Steussie, Todd	T	6-6	318	12/1/70	5	California
77	Stringer, Korey	T	6-4	359	5/8/74	4	Ohio State
83	Tate, Robert	WR	5-10	188	10/19/73	2	Cincinnati
42	Thomas, Orlando	DB	6-1	223	10/21/72	4	Southwestern Louisiana
81	Walsh, Chris	WR	6-1	200	12/12/68	6	Stanford
21	Williams, Moe	RB	6-1	206	7/26/74	3	Kentucky
94	Williams, Tony	DT	6-1	288	7/9/75	2	Memphis
52	Wong, Kailee	LB	6-2	259	5/23/76	R	Stanford

Head Coach: Dennis Green
Assistant Coaches: Hubbard Alexander, wide receivers; Dave Atkins, tight ends; Brian Billick, offensive coordinator; Foge Fazio, defensive coordinator; Jeff Friday, assistant strength and conditioning; Carl Hargrave, running backs; Wade Harman, coaching asst.; Chip Myers, quarterbacks; Tom Olivadotti, inside linebackers; Andre Patterson, defensive line; Richard Solomon, defensive backs; Mike Tice, offensive line; Trent Walters, outside linebackers; Steve Wetzel, strength and conditioning; Gary Zauner, special teams.

Allsport/Jonathan Daniel

Allsport/Matthew Stockman

#96 Jerry Ball
#80 Cris Carter

#7 Randall Cunningham
#26 Robert Smith

Allsport/Tom Pidgeon

Allsport/Tom Hauck

Allsport/Scott Halleran

Allsport/Scott Halleran

#77 Korey Stringer

#86 Jake Reed

#57 Dwayne Rudd

#93 John Randle

Allsport/Scott Halleran

Allsport/Scott Halleran

Allsport/Tom Pidgeon

Allsport/Matthew Stockman

#22 David Palmer

Dennis Green Head Coach

#27 Corey Fuller

#92 Duane Clemons

Allsport/Elsa Hasch

Allsport/Jonathan Daniel

#90 Derrick Alexander
#59 Dixon Edwards

Brian Billick Offensive Coordinator
#84 Randy Moss

Allsport/Stephen Dunn

Allsport/Scott Halleran

Allsport/Scott Halleran

Allsport/Vincent Laforet

Allsport/Brian Bahr

Allsport/Scott Halleran

Allsport/Jonathan Daniel

A PAINFUL HISTORY LESSON

Super Bowl ring could finally remove monkey off Vikings' back

by Roland Lazenby

I t's 1998, and the Minnesota Vikings are on the march again, moving toward the playoffs with the kind of momentum that their fans haven't seen in two decades, not since the days of . . . well, you know, the Great Pain.

Sorry to bring it up, but the Vikings are the only team to lose four Super Bowls without ever having won one. The cliche in the NFL is that thing about having a monkey on your back. The Vikings definitely have the monkey. He's big and purple and mean and full of angst.

Decades of angst.

In the 1970s, if you wanted to think of defense in the NFL, you likely had coach Bud Grant's Vikings in mind. Carl Eller, Jim Marshall, Alan Page and Gary Larsen

made a very mean front four. They were nasty, so nasty that they growled their way to four Super Bowl appearances.

But their nasty visages have been muted by the years and the pain. Today, if you put faces on those old Vikings of the '70s, you probably think of two quarterbacks, Fran Tarkenton and Joe Kapp.

Tarkenton, of course, is a Hall of Famer. Over an 18-year NFL career that spanned stints with the

In Super Bowl IV, Minnesota receiver John Henderson is defended by Kansas City defensive back James Marsalis on a pass from Vikings quarterback Joe Kapp. The Chiefs won 23-7.

Minnesota Vikings, then the New York Giants, then the Viking again, Tarkenton rang up the statistics that make him one of the most prodigious passers in the history o pro football. His yardage gained (47,003), passes completed (3,686), passes attempted (6,467), and touchdown passes (342) stood for a time as the game's records.

Miami Dolphins back Larry Csonka bulls over Vikings cornerback Bobby Bryant during the Dolphins' 24-7 win over Minnesota in Super Bowl VIII.

Tarkenton came to the Vikings, the NFL's newest franchise in 1961, out of the University of Georgia, and he suffered with the team all the growing pains that expansion clubs suffer. Still, they won three games that first year, and by the 1964 season, the Vikings turned in a winner at 8-5-1.

But they stumbled in 1966 and fell to the bottom of the divisional rankings. For 1967, Tarkenton was traded to the New York Giants, where he struggled with a rebuilding team. Tarkenton's departure meant that Bud Grant would have to look elsewhere for some offensive life.

Joe Kapp

In his day, the sportswriters liked to speak of Joe Kapp as a brawling, thuggish competitor, more suited to the bruising existence of an outside linebacker than to the finesse and headiness of a quarterback. Perhaps that's why the defensive-minded Grant liked him.

There was a bit of truth in the depiction. But more than anything, Kapp was a throwback to the days when a quarterback barked signals, blocked with the best of 'em, and never hesitated to lower his head and buck the line for a few extra yards. Basically Kapp did whatever was required to win.

An All-American at California for 1958, he was drafted 18th by the Washington Redskins in the 1959 draft. Rather than face those odds, Kapp took his skills to the Canadian Football League and played there eight seasons until the Vikings took him on as a free agent in 1967.

Opponents and teammates alike marveled at his versatility. "When you're on the football field, you have to use every tool you have," he said simply. "I can't afford to be cautious. I prefer to pass and give the ball to the backs to run. But if a play breaks down and I have to run, yes, I enjoy running."

Those who

Vikings' great Chuck Foreman is met at the line of scrimmage by Miami Dolphins linebacker Nick Buoniconti during the Dolphins' 24-7 victory over Minnesota in Super Bowl VIII.

doubted his passing skills did a double-take early in the 1969 season, when he bombed the defending NFL champions, the Baltimore Colts, for seven touchdowns in a 52-14 rout. His Vikings had lost the first game of the season to the New York Giants, 24-23. Then Minnesota reeled off 12 victories in a row before losing the last game of the regular season, 10-3, to the Atlanta Falcons. They nosed past the Los Angeles Rams in the first round of the playoffs to meet the Cleveland Browns for the NFL championship.

Kapp was masterful in the clutch. He rushed eight times for 57 yards, including a seven-yard touchdown run in the first quarter to open the scoring. On the day,

Vikings quarterback Fran Tarkenton takes the snap from center during Minnesota's 16-6 loss to the Pittsburgh Steelers in Super Bowl IX.

he completed seven of 13 passing attempts for 169 yards, a performance marked by a 75-yard jewel in the first quarter to Gene Washington for a 14-0 lead. He drove the team to 13 more points before Minnesota allowed a single Cleveland touchdown. With the 27-7 victory, the Vikings advanced to the Super Bowl opposite Len Dawson and the Kansas City Chiefs. The Vikings were favored, and although Kapp completed 16 of 25 passing attempts for 183 yards, he also threw two interceptions. Late in the second half, he injured his shoulder and left the game. With a perfect mix of defense and offense, the Chiefs won Super Bowl IV, 23-7, and Vikings fans were left to suffer as victims of the lowly AFL.

Their agony gained the relief of hope when the Vikings re-acquired Tarkenton for the 1972 season. Tarkenton and his teammates found their stride

over the next decade, as the Vikings won their division six straight years and reached the Super Bowl three more times.

Tarkenton was the ultimate scrambler, and as such, he had the image of a gambler out of control. Nothing could be further from the truth. He was a proponent of the controlled, short-pass offense. It fit nicely with the defensive-minded Vikings, and he ran the offense very well.

Tarkenton pushed the team to a 12-2 record and the NFC Central Division title for 1973. He threw two touchdown passes to John Gilliam to beat Washington in the first round of the playoffs, then ran the control offense over Dallas, 27-10, to claim the NFC championship. The Miami Dolphins, however, dominated Super Bowl VII, 24-7, setting up a pattern that would haunt Tarkenton the rest of his career.

The Vikings won the Central again in '74 with a 10-4 record, eliminated St. Louis and Los Angeles in the playoffs on the strength of their defense and control offense, and then struggled against Pittsburgh's defense in Super Bowl IX before losing 16-6. The hurt deepened in Minneapolis and St. Paul, but stranger days were ahead.

Hail Mary

The Vikings were a veteran, balanced team in 1975 and driven to get back to the Super Bowl after having lost pro football's big game the two previous years. Their first obstacle in the playoffs was a young Dallas wild-card team, laced with rookies and carrying a 10-4 record into the game at Metropolitan Stadium in Minneapolis.

A cynic would have said that the up-and-down

Cowboys didn't have a prayer. The day, of course, would prove differently. The Cowboys, in fact, had several prayers. Their late-game miracle would provide the NFL with an Ave Maria for posterity.

The Vikings recovered a fumbled punt in the second quarter and used the field position to take a 7-0 halftime lead. Dallas evened things up with a third-quarter drive, then took the lead on a Toni Fritsch field goal just minutes into the fourth quarter.

Facing the challenge of the season, Tarkenton pulled the Vikings together for a 70-yard drive in 11 plays. Brent McClanahan powered in from the one to make the game 14-10. Faced with a similar challenge,

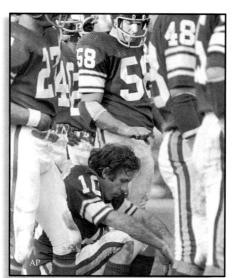

Vikings Hall-of-Famer Fran Tarkenton sits dejected in the final moments of the Vikings' 32-14 loss to the Oakland Raiders in Super Bowl XI. The Vikings haven't returned to the big game since, and remain 0-4 in Super Bowls.

the Cowboy offense fizzled and punted with about three minutes left. Dallas relied on its defense to get the ball back for one last shot. The telling moment came as Minnesota faced a third and two at the Cowboy 47. Tarkenton eschewed the dive for a rollout. Dallas safety Charlie Waters blitzed and dropped him for a three-yard loss. Reluctantly, the Vikings punted.

The Dallas offense again fizzled. The last hope hinged on a fourth-and-16 situation at their own 25. Roger Staubach and receiver Drew Pearson decided to fake a post pattern and angle for the sideline. The momentum of the pass probably would have carried Pearson out of bounds for an incompletion. But he was bumped by cornerback Nate Wright, and the official ruled Pearson had been forced out of bounds.

With 37 seconds left, Dallas had a first down at the 50. When the next pass fell incomplete, Pearson said it was time to work on Wright long again. The pass was short, bringing Pearson back from the end zone to catch it. As he moved to the ball, Wright fell, or as the Vikings claimed, he was knocked down by offensive interference. Pearson caught the ball at the five, clutched it to his waist, then felt it slipping away as he fell into the end zone. With the ball pinned awkwardly at his hip, Pearson glanced around for penalty flags.

There was none, only the dead silence of Metropolitan Stadium. The play became enshrined as "Hail Mary," and has become over the years one of the game's hallowed moments. Tarkenton suffered an even larger loss later, when he learned his father had died of a heart attack watching the game on television.

The Vikings came back strong again in '76, running off an 11-2-1 record and nailing Washington and Los Angeles in the NFC playoffs. Again, Super Bowl XI was an exercise in frustration. The Oakland Raiders dominated, 32-14. Tarkenton left the field in frustration after fumbling in the second half. "We had the emotion," he told reporters later, "but you have to make the big plays to keep it going."

Injuries kept Tarkenton out of the NFC championship game in '77, and the Dallas Cowboys shoved the Vikings aside there, 24-7. Minnesota won the Division the next season, Tarkenton's last, but his final Super Bowl hopes died in the first round of the playoffs at the hands of the Los Angeles Rams, 34-10.

Three times Tarkenton had taken a fine team to within one game of the world championship. That and his passing records would have to be his consolation. For those great achievements, Tarkenton was voted into the Hall of Fame in 1986.

For Vikings fans, the agony hasn't faded with the passing of time. In fact, the monkey has grown with season after season of frustration through the '80s and '90s. Is it time for Randall Cunningham and company to change all that? That's just the question that has all of Minnesota going bananas. ■